THE PRIEST AND VOCATIONS

IN THE SAME SERIES

RELIGIOUS LIFE

XI

THE PRIEST
AND VOCATIONS

Translated by

RONALD HALSTEAD

AQUIN PRESS LONDON

First published as
Le Role du Pretre dans L'Eveil des Vocations
Les Editions du Cerf, Paris 1958

© 1961 by Aquin Press

Nihil obstat: Daniel Duivesteijn, S.T.D.
Censor deputatus
Imprimatur: E. Morrogh Bernard
Vic. Gen.
Westmonasterii, die 29a Septembris, 1961

The *Nihil obstat* and *Imprimatur* are a
declaration that a book or pamphlet is
considered to be free from doctrinal or
moral error. It is not implied that those
who have granted the *Nihil obstat* and *Imprimatur* agree with the contents, opinions
or statements expressed

Printed in Great Britain by
The Garden City Press Limited
Letchworth, Hertfordshire

CONTENTS

LETTER FROM MGR BROT

Paris, 6th June, 1957.

Dear Reverend Father,

I wholeheartedly approve your desire to present the account of the proceedings of the 1956 Congress to the priests of France, and I congratulate you.

The large number of our brethren who attended these days of prayer and study is proof of the interest they have aroused; and all those who were present profited by the exchange of views which followed the conferences.

The priest has an extremely important role in discerning and awakening vocations to the religious life. Today, when evangelisation is the concern of every Christian, it is the urgent duty of priests, as they apply themselves to the instruction of the corps d'élite of Catholic Action in every parish, to put due emphasis on the religious life, and to help those souls whom God is calling to a life entirely devoted to his service to respond to their vocation.

Undoubtedly God can act directly, and inspire a young girl with the desire for greater sanctification by consecrating herself to him, by being an apostle . . . but then his call often comes circumspectly as well, and it falls to the priest to help the soul to discern it, to enlighten the understanding, to dispose the will, and to prepare her to respond to the divine invitation.

It is a delicate task, demanding shrewd psychology, an immense supernatural prudence on the part of the priest, and requiring a thorough knowledge and appreciation of the religious life.

Several eminent members of the Conference with reason expressed the hope that the study of the States of Perfection might find a place in the teaching of theology at the seminaries.

vii

I hope, Reverend Father, that the lessons of this book may be approved and put into practice by those many priests who have the extension of the Kingdom of God and the exaltation of Holy Church at heart.

Please accept, Reverend Father, this expression of my gratitude and my devoted respect in Our Lord and Our Lady.

PIERRE BROT,

Bishop of Marciame
Co-Adjutor to the Union of
Superiors General of France.

PREFACE

AMONG THE resolutions passed at the conclusion of the first National Conference for Priests ministering to Religious in September 1953,[1] and approved by the Assembly of Cardinals and Archbishops, was the intention that such conferences should be held every three years. The second was therefore held in September 1956 under the presidency of the Rt Rev. Mgr Pierre Brot, a member of the Episcopal Commission for Religious, at the Grand Seminaire d'Issay-les-Moulineaux.

Like the previous conference it was organised in collaboration with all the various bodies concerned with religious life in France and its theme was the role of the priest in fostering vocations to the religious life. This theme was chosen not only because it presents urgent and difficult problems but also because it emphasises a point of law which is not sufficiently appreciated in practice: that not only wardens and chaplains but *all* priests, both secular and regular, have responsibilities towards Religious. All of them in effect have, or will have, to exercise their ministry under one from or another with Religious. This is particularly true in respect of the awakening of vocations.

No priest can remain indifferent to the urgent need of the whole Church for an improvement in the number and quality of the 'brides of Christ'. And this apostolic solicitude must be aroused in the priest; he must be enlightened in the principles and encouraged in the practice of this ministry, which is both delicate and indispensable. From the time of the awakening of a girl's religious vocation to her becoming a postulant, the priest has a part to play. Do priests really realise this? Are they sufficiently well instructed to perform this ministry properly?

In organising this conference and publishing the reports given there we have no purpose other than to help our brethren in the priesthood not to neglect, mentally at any rate, any of the obligations of their office in Church of Christ.

FR A. PLÉ, O.P.

The Direction of Nuns, Aquin Press.

PART ONE

PRINCIPLES

CHAPTER I

CLERICAL PREJUDICES CONCERNING NUNS

AT THE beginning of this first conference of the second National Congress of Priests ministering to Religious I think it necessary to make three points concerning:

1. The place of this paper in the programme as a whole.
2. The aim of this paper.
3. The person of the speaker.

1. The place of this paper

Your time here is to be devoted to a consideration of the active part played by the priest in the awakening of vocations to the religious life. But it is first necessary to remove or at any rate to define the obstacles which might prevent him from carrying out this work.

To study clerical prejudices concerning nuns is to examine the attitude of mind of the clergy to them; an attitude which you, of course, do not share, but which many of your brethren do, and I think you ought not to lose sight of it during our time here, if our work is to correct and construct something in the Church of God, and not merely to be a fruitless recital of facts.

2. The aim of this paper

I am going to deal with 'Clerical prejudices concerning nuns: Causes. Remedies'. In the first part, I am going to speak of these prejudices, and make incursions into the realm of psychology to discover the mental attitude behind them. I certainly do not pretend that my work is exhaustive, but on this point it will have the advantage —and this is its only real value—of being the summary of very extensive inquiries and a variety of consultations.

For the second part, in which I shall consider both causes and remedies I make even fewer claims to completeness. I shall content myself with giving you the result of my own reflections on the facts as shown by analysis, and with grouping these very simple deductions

3

together to serve as pointers and signposts which your days of study might profitably follow.

3. The person of the speaker

In asking a bishop to give this opening conference you have automatically ensured that it shall have a diocesan slant, that it will be a consideration of the mental attitude of the diocesan clergy towards those religious they meet with in the course of their daily ministry—teaching, parochial and nursing sisters. So it is not within my scope, nor will it be possible, to consider the prejudices of the regular clergy, nor to deal with the attitudes of mind of the secular clergy towards monks.

This defines clearly the limits of my subject.

I   PREJUDICES OF THE DIOCESAN CLERGY CONCERNING NUNS

I shall begin my catalogue with those criticisms which bear on the practice of the apostolate, and go on to those which touch the person of the religious herself. Or, in philosophical language, I shall proceed from the *opus religiosum* to the *esse religiosum*.

A. THE PRACTICE OF THE APOSTOLATE

I shall speak first about teaching, because of the special position of religious devoting themselves to this work, and because of the importance and weight of the evidence received. Then I shall consider all the other forms of activity performed by religious—nursing, social work, or their more strictly parochial duties.

1. The teaching sister

We have to distinguish at the very outset the boarding schools and high schools from the ordinary parochial schools.

(a) Boarding and High Schools

The replies reveal a disturbing unanimity—in general these establishments are ivory towers, from which the direct and positive influence of the diocesan clergy is jealously excluded, and which, to all intents and purposes, detach the best elements from the parish and train them, as it were, in a 'glass case'. They then send them back to their parishes ill-adapted, apart from the rare exception, to parochial service and the most valuable and authentic parochial activities, in short, to the concrete apostolic tasks which attract the young girl of today who is desirous of rising to her vocation as a lay-woman within the Church.

There appear to be two reasons for this.

First, the instruction given her is insufficiently in touch with reality, with things that matter; it is too attached to methods which are described as 'tried', which perhaps envisage the fostering of some vocations for the Congregation rather than the training of young people, the majority of whom are not destined for the cloister—far from it!

In the second place, there is the question of the *religious* instruction given to the children—it is deficient, precisely because the priest does not play a large enough part in it; it is given by religious who do not possess the necessary theological and biblical learning, and who, under cover of the 'grace of their state', make do with improvisation, and do not get beyond a stereotyped teaching which is lacking in missionary vision and apostolic outlook. In short, a religious training which produces 'practising members' rather then 'Christians', a piety which is sentimental and transient rather than a deep and living faith.

The teaching congregation is concerned to train children who will really posses the spirit of the Order—its stamp;—so much so that the pupils of one establishment will scarcely mix with those of other establishments, even at meetings such as J.M.F., art classes and youth-clubs, even if they live in the same district or even in the same street. The Order will have its old girls who will naturally be called upon to take up teaching appointments there because they possess its spirit, but if other Christian teachers, trained at another house or the products of another system, apply and have to be considered, a certain reserve will be shown towards them, and they will be associated only at a distance with the apostolic preoccupations of the establishment.

So both the parish priest, observing the mental attitudes of these young pupils, his parishioners, and receiving the confidences of their Christian teachers as well, and also the curate who maintains and inspires a little group of young actionists, will wonder if this particular institution is capable of producing the yeast to leaven the girlhood of the parish as a whole.

(b) The Parochial Schools

The parish priest obviously feels more at home here, for these schools are in varying degrees dependent on him and under his control.

They are his responsibility, and this gives rise to his fundamental complaint about the religious. I have been teaching and mingling in teaching circles too long not to know that children are not educated by improvisation, lack of organisation and 'making-do'. Hence a tendency on the part of the religious, who spends nothing on herself, to spend freely where the school is concerned. There are excellent religious who, prompted by the vow of poverty, will make an effort to light the altar candles with the same match every morning, but who have not realised that things cannot be changed or obtained at once simply because 'the school needs them'. Classrooms are repainted, new tables ordered, a new teacher engaged—as if these things were to be taken for granted because 'the school needs them', and then the bill is presented to the parish priest after the event.

But the chief complaint is often the lack of general culture or of preparation for teaching, a far too elementary catechistical instruction; and above all, perhaps, the absence of open and frank co-operation. We are not working as a team and in the open.

The parish priest cannot see why a diocesan congregation meant for both teaching and hospital work allows his anxious appeal to go unanswered, when he will have to close a school if he does not obtain teaching personnel, yet this congregation maintains numerous religious serving a hospital or a clinic; he does not understand why, in his parish, a magnificent building shelters a few old ladies who board there, while almost next door his free school is bursting out of its cramped quarters. So he is led to infer—and it is a pity, since he does not possess the facts with which to form a judgment, and to voice his opinion—which, again, is a pity—that the interests of the Church do not always appear to be the first to be served.

2. Other apostolic tasks of the religious

I come now, *per modum unius*, to the prejudices of the diocesan clergy about religious serving the parishes in various other tasks—the hospitals, social welfare, instruction, etc. At the outset I should like to ignore sweeping and superficial judgments; the clergy easily indulge in and repeat slogans, very often aimed at the government of superiors or the differing spiritualities of the congregations. A single religious will be quoted, and by her the whole religious life is judged and assessed; or again, young women who have left the convent will be quoted—and these often find a perfect and uncritical audience (especially in their former director of conscience)—yet it is probably because they were incapable of any deep understanding of the religious life that they did not stay.

However, if I pick out a few quotations from a collection which is, unhappily, inexhaustible, it is because by starting with these, we shall be able to get at the real complaints.

A girl informs her J.I.C. chaplain that she is to enter such and such a congregation, which is actually quite unknown to him. He replies: 'All communities have routine in plenty; try to find two or three companions to join you in opposing what you will be told and asked —and brush the cobwebs off these establishments'.

A director answered one of his spiritual children in these words: 'If you enter the religious life, after two or three months you will be no longer capable of uttering more than "Amen" to anything your superior asks of you'.

In the 'Answers to Correspondents' columns in a periodical on Spirituality which reaches hundreds of girls, we read in answer to the question 'Why do girls from Catholic Action have more difficulty than others in adapting themselves to the religious life?': 'This is quite normal, as religious establishments are antiquated, tied to routine, not flexible. . . . So, naturally, fervent and generous young people will suffer in them. Yet it is really a good thing for young and vigorous blood to enter and revivify these semi-corpses, and the congregations cannot but benefit from this infusion. As for the young people themselves, they should be aware of the duty awaiting them; to brush off the old cobwebs they will find there, and make all things new.'

These extravagant statements reveal the fundamental prejudices, which can be indicated by these three words—inadaption, individualism and authoritarianism. (I wonder if religious would not readily mention these very same points if they were asked to disclose their own prejudices about the clergy!)

(a) Inadaption to the Apostolate

First, because their obedience puts an end to receptivity, nuns often imagine they are dispensed from thinking, from looking at problems squarely and deeply. They always remain minors to those superiors

2—TPAV

who reserve the thinking to themselves, and alone represent their congregations on the various commissions and working committees. Hence, they are lacking in breadth of outlook, in appreciation of human problems, and are unaware of social and moral questions. They have a poor understanding of the actual lives of the laity, and in particular of the advances made by the working class, or of its mentality. Good will and sanctity are no substitutes for an understanding of people, or for a conscience awakened to the demands of justice. Religious in hospitals do not grasp the drama of the situation when the wage-earner's wife, the mother of a large family, falls ill; and the head of a clinic will scarcely desire the organisation of a group of J.O.C.F. or of a 'trades union movement' among her employees.

We will also mention that the habit is objected to, as a hindrance to apostolic action—'What would not be asked of you, if it were not for your habit!'

(b) Apostolic Authoritarianism

The religious tends to keep responsibility too much in her own hands, and lacks faith in the personal capabilities of youth in general, and working-class youth in particular. She has a tendency to project her spiritual maternity on to the natural plane—hence a maternalism, a seeking to influence and to 'direct'; a permanent temptation to make cliques, to project her own vocation on to young people with less personality, and to coax them when the time comes for them to leave boarding school.

(c) Apostolic Individualism

Vows, Constitutions, the Rule and its Horarium render the religious less versatile and 'available' than a lay person for those many things one would like her to undertake. She always gives the impression —perhaps unconsciously—of working for her congregation, and of not being over-anxious to 'work with'—*with* the parochial clergy (not enough simplicity or plain speaking in her co-operation with the priest), *with* others responsible for work with children, *with* Catholic Action movements, *with* parents and family groups.

A director of an apostolic Organisation subscribed to this statement: 'Religious perform their good works, but do not enter into the common Work'.

B. The Person of the Religious

It is time to suspend, or rather to proceed beyond, our analysis of the nun's apostolic activities, and to take up the subject of the prejudices of the clergy concerning her person and her state of life.

It is a fact that the priest thinks highly of the religious life in general. It is a fact that the priest speaks with admiration of such and such a religious with whom he came into contact in the course of his ministry. But it is also a fact that the priest shows considerable reticence about religious houses, the instruction given in them and the kind of life imposed on their subjects.

Think of one of his own young parishioners and penitents who enters the convent. Here is a child, so spontaneous and 'direct', who is going to lose all the marks of her personality, including her own style and writing. Obedience will vow her to infantilism, and rob her of all her own characteristic reactions. A faculty professor claimed that for those of his students who were religious, a book would be interesting if the Mother Superior had said so. . . . She is not going to acquire the spirit of poverty, but mere frugality, until chastity makes her cold-hearted and old before her time.

What do they say about the common life, which, because of human peevishness and pettiness, is such a wonderful test: 'making mountains out of molehills'? They don't love one another, they tolerate one another by endurance; they don't pray, they say prayers.

So, then, this form of life seems to the priest to be a kind of infidelity; infidelity to the evangelical spirit, because the ideal, clothed in soulless and petrified rules, is robbed of its savour, and everything is given the same importance; infidelity to the world of today, because so many Orders are unadapted to the demands of a Christianity which is concerned with authentic and absolute religious values.

However, this lack of adaptation on the part of the religious communities has been fully discussed, as well as their inability to give that witness which the modern age is waiting for. It is increasingly suggested that the old Orders and Congregations have had their day, and that modern life demands forms more versatile and aware; it is a point which is continually being taken up by well-intentioned journals in investigations, interviews and articles, which see in this outlook 'the demands of modern youth, and the mournful cry of a frustrated hope'. But we have learnt from the studies of the last ten years that problems as serious as this are not to be dragged into the market place, for their solution is not to be found there.

Meanwhile, preachers of retreats for the young are presenting marriage in its highest aspect—and this is indeed a cause for rejoicing—but they are finding it inopportune to speak of the vocation to the religious life, and declare with evident good faith 'that in our day it is very difficult to orientate to the religious life young girls who are intelligent, dynamic and alert to spiritual realities, because convent life stifles them'.

This is a grim picture, but I have not systematically exaggerated or blackened it; once again, all these points are taken from genuine and sincere statements. Remember, Reverend Fathers, you have religious in your charge, and so you are acquainted with the religious life from the inside, you are familiar with its essential features; and you have come together here for three days to consider the role of the priest in the awakening of vocations—and that is a very fine thing. But you must realise that the priest we must consider is that rector, that curate, that Guide or Catholic Action chaplain who shares the prejudices we have just mentioned. Consequently, it is a priest such as this that you must keep in mind during these three days, and it is up to you to make known the points which I shall speak of here. So we must go on to ask why this priest thinks as he does, and we shall then be on the way to putting things right.

II CAUSES AND REMEDIES

A little quiet reflection, in the spirit of faith, will enable us to distinguish the fundamental outlines of the preceding premises, and to advance some positive deductions from them.

Of course, an investigation into causes and remedies reveals a bilateral problem: the problem of the religious, and the problem of the priest; but I shall restrict myself to a consideration of the question so far as it concerns the diocesan clergy, and I shall only give explanations which you have already heard. But do not pass over them too quickly. It is rather a disadvantage of these Conferences that they are apt to make us think that views are changed and errors corrected, merely because they have been diagnosed and denounced.

Why, then, do the diocesan clergy think as they do? I will give three very simple reasons. In practice, the diocesan clergy do not really understand:

1. What women are
2. What religious are
3. That a woman, by virtue of being a religious, has a special position in the Church.

A. FEMININITY

Is this point, which is none the less essential, too elementary or too delicate to be mentioned?

It is possible to do this in the way a newspaper reporter does when he claims to be giving to the public at large 'a sensational revelation' of the mysterious life of nuns and sisters, and begins by declaring that 'religious are women; more so, indeed, than others . . . creatures of flesh, because all and always vulnerable; crushed by a mode of life which seems—and is—abnormal, today more than formerly. . . .' And if he returns to this point in his story, it is to correct it: 'Actually, not quite women . . . old maids'.

It is understandable that such assumptions of a naturistic psychology should deeply wound religious souls.

But this matter of femininity can also be presented with the pastoral penetration of the Bishop of Chartres, who, when dealing with the subject of collaboration between clergy and religious at the Congress de l'Union des Oeuvres (Versailles 1956) said:

'The priest and the religious are man and woman, with their profoundly different psychologies; the one sees things on a vast canvas, grasps things as a whole, while the other tends rather to see details; one moves in the abstract, the other more naturally in the concrete; one is above all logical, the other intuitive. . . . All this can be the source of enrichment, when there is collaboration, for these differences are by way of being complementary; but too often, because of their respective training, there is either ignorance or misunderstanding. The soul of a woman remains, to a varying degree, a dark mystery which it is difficult for the priestly mind to penetrate.'

Or again, this femininity could be presented as a 'diptych', in the way Sister Marie of the Redemption portrayed with such profound intuition the psychological make-up of the religious, at your first national Conference in 1953; on one side, the picture of the religious, obviously happy, liberated and unified by the greatest possible love of a God who first loved her; on the other side, the picture of the religious subject to the failings inherent in her feminine temperament, which permit recurrences of the attacks of nature. Indeed—and *this* is her trial—for as long as she is travelling the road of perfection here on earth, the religious will be living more or less on both these levels the whole time.

She is a woman, and hence a weak creature who naturally experiences the need for someone to lean on, the desire for someone to be interested in her, which may lead to simulation and duplicity.

She is a woman, and hence she possesses a practical, analytical mind, running the risk of getting lost in details, or of putting everything on the same level of importance, at the same time as an imagination which tends to exaggerate, to distort, to fabricate.

She is a woman; her emotional make-up is such that she feels the need to love and to be loved.

What does the priest know of all this? Of course, he has been told about it and he has read it in books, but whatever he thinks and proclaims, he knows little about the feminine temperament before sitting in the Confessional, or coming into contact with women's organisations and religious communities. And it is a pity.

Could not the advanced seminarist occasionally be put in touch with the leaders of women's organisations, mothers of families, religious? They would tell him what they do and what they are, and the future priest would then find out in concrete fashion about 'those differences which are by way of being complementary . . . and which can be a source of enrichment when there is collaboration'.

I think a great step forward on the way to apostolic co-operation would be taken if priests were in practice more receptive to the idea of the complementary nature of these differences.

There are innumerable examples. We will simply take that of catechistical teaching, since in this era of dechristianisation this ministry is to be considered as 'the most sacred and the most necessary of all', to quote the Holy Father's words,—'the most sacred duty in the vocation of a teaching sister'.

Thus a pastor will appeal to the religious, because he is overwhelmed by the number of children, to take his place with some of them, whereas they should both have their place with them all, as complementary to each other; and if the parish only contains a small number of children of catechism age, the same pastor will see no need at all to seek the help of the religious. Shall we one day learn that we cannot form Christians—children who are going to live the faith, and who are not going to throw it all over the same day as their First Communion—without the co-operation of the community of the family, and the community of the parish? But where this necessary co-operation does not exist, because the family and the community of the parish fall short, the religious will supply the deficiency through her 'complementary' nature. She will be a clear-sighted substitute who does not accept the situation. The religious knows that this 'maternal suppliance' must aim at fostering other forms of motherhood—that of the family, and that of the Church, of which the parochial community is the effective sign.

Do we look at it like this? Do we co-operate with the religious in this way, which is her own because she is a woman?

B. THE CONSECRATED STATE

Here, we can say without hesitation that the priest does not understand the religious.

What did we learn at the seminary? We studied the canonical aspect of the religious state from some treatise on moral theology, but at the time when our minds and hearts were eager for spiritual nourishment, the religious life was not presented as something deeply rooted in the mystery of Christ. The essence of the religious life, the meaning of consecrated virginity, the spiritual significance of the religious vows, their mystical, apostolic and eschatological value—all these essential principles, which should today be guiding our judgments and moulding our opinions, remained abstract, superficial, and without influence on our priesthood.

It would be interesting to know what place has been given to the encyclical *Sacra Virginitas* in the seminaries and at priests' conferences during the past three years. What works has it prompted, what teaching and preaching has it inspired?

An impoverished idea of the religious life—an idea empty of any real content—clearly arouses but an indifferent zeal for awakening and fostering vocations.

Nor does it make contacts and exchanges between priest and religious any easier. The superior, coming to the conclusion that the priest is acquainted neither with the principles nor the exigencies of the religious life, will be tempted to withdraw her little community from his influence, perhaps even from the influence of his confessional . . . and, on the other hand, I notice the confusion of the parish priest when asked by his parochial sisters to give them a monthly conference—what on earth is he to say to them?

I am not going to develop the theology of the religious state here. (Oh, if only we had studied in our seminary days those questions which treat of the various states of life.) I only want to indicate one aspect, essential to our subject, the lack of appreciation of which is the source of many misunderstandings, grievances and prejudices concerning religious prevalent among the clergy.

The religious life is not primarily a *convenient state for service*, but a *state of consecration*.

Throughout the Old Testament we observe this hallowing of life and of the circumstances of life, of space and time, of years and days, of the earth and its crops, of fruits and animals, and of a man's first-born child. It was by this consecrating that Israel preserved the sense of the sacred, the sense of the Only God and of the mission of his chosen people. Then came the day when that dedicated First-born, duly consecrated by the Presentation in the Temple which ratified the Crib and foretold the Cross, was not redeemed. Thenceforward, those 'who follow the Lamb whithersoever he goeth' are freely placed in a state of consecration, and it is through these consecrated souls, mingling like living and visible leaven with the mass of mankind, that the world will preserve a sense of what is the source and strength of their consecration—the consecration of the Mass and the consecration of the Cross.

More than ever before, our world has need of this witness, to preserve or rediscover a sense of the sacred, the sense of God as the Absolute, and of man as the Relative.

It is only natural that, with the needs of the hour in mind, some priests should desire the creation of religious organisations which would be more 'aware', more flexible; but do they think that everything has been said when they have spoken of 'commando-religious'? For we must not think that the existing orders and congregations could offer this flexibility and 'awareness'. It is all very romantic to see the modern religious as a new version of St Cecilia, living in a garret of some hotel in Montmartre and confidentially revealing her divine espousals to some Valerian of the Faubourg. But these are quite exceptional vocations, like the spearheads of an army, and they are secure in the knowledge that they can always fall back on the main body behind them.

There is one conclusion we can draw from this—that in practice the clergy dismiss the state of consecration of the religious in favour of her state of service. 'I need one sister for my school; I need two sisters for my parish.' So what happens here and there—and there is a tendency to it everywhere—is that one or two sisters are performing some service, true enough, but, because the strength of a living community is lacking, are in many cases no longer furnishing that leaven of consecration which people expect of them.

We shall never know to what extent we have wronged the religious life, and deprived consecrated souls of light in thus destroying 'organised houses'. But what can superiors do in face of our entreaties? With an empty novitiate, and perhaps but five or six religious, they release one or two of them, and thus do their religious life a great wrong; that policy which has sought to counter the lack of vocations not by closing houses, but by keeping them going without the necessary elements, has been disastrous for the religious life and recruitment to it.

C. THE POSITION OF THE RELIGIOUS IN THE CHURCH

We know well enough that the Church comprises ecclesiastical Hierarchy, Religious and Laity, but do we know what place the religious sister holds within this Church, which, as an entity, must become a missionary Church to face the growing dechristianisation of the masses? What position and functions have been assigned to her?

This question was actually raised by Mgr Blanchet at the Congrès Général des Religieuses in June 1954, and quite recently the auxiliary bishop of Malines, Mgr Suenens, in his book *L'Église en état de mission* has devoted a chapter to it, which is of the greatest interest.

Our consideration of this question has been much encouraged by that official inspiration which has come from Rome, and which has been given such a splendid welcome by religious—the creation of the various national commissions in a great effort of adaptation.

The impetus and directives have been given by the Sacred Congregation of Religious in the name of the Sovereign Pontiff, and there has been a generous response on the part of religious; what remains to be done is on the diocesan level. Here there are three objectives:

1. Unification—which does not mean diverting the various congregations from their own particular vocations, but, in the fellowship of charity, helping them to look at the Bishop's plan of evangelisation together, and together to take their part in it.

2. Integration into the life of Catholic Action—the religious must have a place in this. Mgr Suenens quotes Pius XI's words: 'The duty of winning the laity for Catholic Action is an integral part of the vocation of a religious.' The function of the religious is, then, complementary to that of the priest in rousing the laity to missionary activity.

3. Direct missionary work. Mgr Suenens refers to these words from Abbé Michonneau:

'As things are now, we have flourishing Orders doing almost every conceivable kind of work, ranging from orphanages to hospitals. Not for one moment would we even hint that this work is not valuable; it is indeed, and we would be lost without it. But, if there were a Congregation which would devote itself exclusively to a door to door preaching of Christ, without any secondary motive, we believe that a tremendous uprising of Christianity would result. Everyone accepts nuns, and respects them. In lay or religious dress, they could be the Christian equivalent of social workers, or the Western equivalent of mission catechists; better still, they could provide the Catholic equivalent of the evangelical zeal of the Salvation Army.'[1]

Behind that statement is the truth that religious do not usually adjust themselves easily to direct missionary work, in regional missions, for example. Is it not our job to help them to do so?

This seems to me to be of special importance in providing the answer to the most oft-repeated grievance, that the religious, in practice at any rate, does not *sentire cum Ecclesia*, that she does not put the interests of the Church first, above those of her congregation. But have we really helped her to find her place in the Church?

Believe me, fathers and brethren, the diocesan clergy have still much to do to discharge their obligations and responsibilities to religious.

HIS EXCELLENCY MGR FERRAND,
Archbishop of Tours.

---

[1] *Revolution in a City Parish*, Michonneau, Aquin Press.

CHAPTER II

THE NATURE OF THE DIVINE CALL IN
RELIGIOUS VOCATION

THERE ARE some creatures God seems to reserve for himself alone. The priest, who realises this, is filled with respect for them. It is God who is calling them. At heart the mystery of vocation is this, that God lays his hand upon certain persons so that they shall live for him and his work alone.

I should like to define the nature of this call, and to do so shall

(i) look at religious vocation within the mystery of God, its author
(ii) attempt to bring out its particular object
(iii) examine its form.

I RELIGIOUS VOCATION IS GROUNDED IN THE MYSTERY OF GOD,
ITS AUTHOR

Here I should like simply to note three general marks of God's call. It is supremely free. It is destined for Christ and his Church. It is incorporated into the very being of the person called.

A. It seemed to me of capital importance to emphasise strongly at the very outset the supernatural and inherently mysterious aspect of a vocation. It confronts us with a divine initiative of the supernatural order. This means that in the last analysis it will always elude us. We can certainly recount the history of a vocation, and examine the stages of its development, but in the end we shall be confronted with the absolutely unfettered design of God, which we can only adore. He has been pleased to create us. He has been pleased to call us, in his Son, to this or that end, and we cannot call him to account.

We know how St Paul made himself the great Doctor of the Liberty of God, who calls whom he will (Rom. 9, 15–17). The magnificent text which follows undoubtedly envisages Christian vocation, vocation to faith and to baptism, but it sheds its own sharp light upon all vocation, and, therefore, upon religious vocation.

17

'And we know that to them that love God all things work together unto good, to such as according to his purpose are called to be saints. For whom he foreknew, he also predestinated to be made conformable to the image of his Son, that he might be the firstborn amongst many brethren. And whom he predestinated, them he also called; and whom he called, them he also justified; and whom he justified, them he also glorified' (Rom. 8, 28–30).

Every vocation is thus contingent on the mystery of predestination. And for this predestination, who can give reasons?

God calls whom he will: 'You have not chosen me, but I have chosen you' (John 15, 16), and St Mark expressly observes, on the choosing of the Twelve, that 'going up into a mountain, he called unto him whom he would' (Mark 3, 13).

B. But sovereign liberty does not mean caprice. God's call always comes with a very definite end in view. On this point, study of the Scriptures shows us that this end is always Christ and his Church. The mystery of vocation, in the Holy Bible, is fundamentally the vocation of Israel as the people of God, in itself proclaiming the Christ and his Church.

C. Finally, the call of God does not come accidentally to the person called; it actually constitutes the very substance of his being. Here again, study of the Scriptures shows us that the mystery of vocation is bound up with that of creation. God calls in creating, and he creates for a definite vocation. 'Jacob, my servant, and Israel whom I have chosen. Thus saith the Lord that made and formed thee . . . from the womb' (Isaias 44, 1). 'But when it pleased him who separated me from my mother's womb and called me by his grace to reveal his Son in me' (Gal. 1, 15).

So if the mystery of vocation is hidden in the mystery of the Liberty of God, it is also hidden in the mystery of our birth and of our creation, and it is incorporated into the very substance of our being.

At the end of this short exposition we are thus able to draw three very significant conclusions.

1. Vocation is a mystery itself hidden in that of Divine Predestination. When we are faced with this, only one attitude is fitting—that of prayer and humility. 'Be it done to me according to thy word.'

It is a question of discovering, humbly, if God is calling—and of that alone.

2. No vocation is solely for the benefit of him who is the object of it. It has Christ and his Church in view. Only one attitude is fitting here, too—that of the servant. It is a question of discovering how, to ensure

salvation, one can best serve God and his Church—and of that alone.

3. Vocation is incorporated into our being. So it is in our inmost self, as made by God, that we must read it.

Once again, only one attitude is fitting—that of fidelity to that inmost self, even at its most demanding. It is a question of doing what God has created us for—and of that alone.

But why has he made us? What is the purpose of his call?

II   THE PARTICULAR OBJECT OF GOD'S CALL IN VOCATION

A. First of all, with St Paul, we must state our fundamental vocation to faith and baptism. 'One body, and one Spirit, as you are called in one hope of your vocation; One Lord, one faith, one baptism' (Eph. 4, 4–5). So our really fundamental vocation is that of our baptism. All the others are differentiations of its potentialities.

About this vocation to faith and baptism, I would like simply to

1. emphasise that it is *the vocation* in the full and proper sense of the word.

2. attempt to define its object.

1. The teaching of the Holy Books is unanimous. St Paul and St Peter reserve the term 'the elect' for those who, by a very special grace, have been called to the knowledge of the Christian mystery. In point of fact, the vast universe obeys the laws of the Creator. He calls the stars and they say: 'Here we are'. But the New Testament does not use the word 'call' in connection with the natural order. It always reserves this word to designate 'a personal and incommunicable call which, out of sheer grace and in utter freedom, the Heavenly Father addresses to a man's heart, to reveal his Son to him'.

'Vocation', in the language of the New Testament, is really used to indicate a mystery, in the very exact sense which theology later gave to this term—i.e. a reality which is not revealed in the natural course of things, but which is reserved to God, and proper to him, which is, in the natural order of things, incommunicable to any creature. Christian vocation thus places us at the centre of an essentially supernatural mystery of Liberty and of Love, by which God calls a creature to know his Son. 'Blessed art thou, Simon Bar-Jona; because flesh and blood hath not revealed it to thee, but my Father who is in heaven' (Matt. 16, 17).

When we come to speak of vocation to the religious life, we have to ask ourselves if we must reserve the term 'vocation', in this proper and strict sense, to it as well.

2. What, precisely, is the object of Christian vocation?

To take up the words of holy scripture, it is to know 'the riches of the glory of this mystery among the Gentiles, which is Christ, in you the hope of glory' (Col. 1, 27); or 'to comprehend, with all the saints, what is the breadth and length and height and depth; to know also the charity of Christ' (Eph. 3, 19). In short, it is to know Christ and to be united with him. So vast is this object that we can understand why the Apostles could not use the word 'vocation' for any other reality. It was *the* call, *the* vocation per excellence, the fulfilment of all other 'calls'—the vocation to know Christ.

The object of Christian vocation, then, is to 'know' Christ, with that supernatural knowledge which is a gift of God through a lively faith, and which is normally given expression in baptism. But this object itself—to know Christ—seems to have two sides to it. This is supported by the passage in Mark 3, 14, where, on the subject of the vocation of the twelve Apostles, the Evangelist notes that the Lord 'made that twelve should be with him and that he might send them to preach'. We observe here two inseparable principles in the vocation of the Apostles—to be 'with the Lord', and to be 'sent to preach'. Can we say that, basically, baptism embraces both these principles—belonging to Christ, and mission for Christ? Let us try to be more specific.

The principle of belonging to Christ implies something which is supremely personal, intimate, incommunicable; something pertaining to the order of sanctity. Whatever the actual words employed—'to know God' (St John), 'to be conformed to Christ' (St Paul)—the reality is the same: to penetrate ever more deeply into the mystery of Christ. Whatever the particular vocation might be, in the grace of baptism there is always, first and fundamentally, a call to sanctity, which experience teaches us can be attained wherever God wills, by the mother of a family as well as by a Carmelite.

The principle of 'mission' is seen rather as something pertaining to the ministerial order, and concerns particular 'ministries' in the Body of Christ. We shall remember how Mgr Cerfaux, in his work on *The Church according to St Paul*, divides the various ministries or charismata into those of mercy, of non-hierarchical teaching, exceptional charismata and hierarchical charismata. At all events, it seems certain that every baptised person, by the very fact of his baptism, is called to some service, some 'ministry' in the Church; and as he is called by his baptism to continual growth in interior knowledge of Christ, so he is called by that same baptism to give himself increasingly to a particular service in the Church.

If this view is correct, then baptismal grace is deployed into a two-fold stream giving rise to a twofold vocation, one aspect of which we can describe as 'a vocation of belonging to Christ', and the other as 'a ministerial vocation'. Religious vocations come in the first category—i.e. of belonging to Christ. Apostolic vocations, and therefore the vocation to the priesthood, fall into the second—i.e. service within the Church. Of course, there is constant exchange between these two types. But it certainly does seem that there are two distinct 'directions', giving rise to two distinct vocations—on the one hand a vocation which pertains rather to the order of sanctity and which reveals itself by way of interior call, and on the other, a vocation which belongs more properly to the ministerial order and which reveals itself rather by way of hierarchial mission.

B. We can now define the real object of the religious vocation. It is to be found in baptism, in that principle of 'belonging to Christ', or to use another expression, in the evangelical *sequere me*, which merely makes the 'belonging' more specific, and carries it to its logical conclusion. Now, as we know, this evangelical principle of the *Sequela Christi* is dominated by the appeal of the evangelical counsels. It is in the acceptance of every letter of the evangelical counsels that the characteristic mark of the vocation to the religious life is to be found.

Here we have to recall that the evangelical counsels are proposals, appeals made by the Lord that those great boons which men normally seek, family love, property, legitimate independence, should be given up in order to follow him more closely. Catholic doctrine on this point has distinguished the letter of the counsels, which consists in effective detachment from these things which are in themselves good, from the spirit of the counsels, which consists in an interior detachment and in a facility effectively to free oneself from them if God should so demand. It has likewise defined that the spirit of the counsels is inseparable from the growth of charity—there can be no sanctity without their constant appeal. On the other hand, the letter of the counsels is not necessary to the growth of charity, and that is why it is merely recommended, and not imposed; but because of the infirmity of our hearts, which so easily become wrapped up in creatures, it is counselled by the Lord as the narrow, and normally higher, way which will lead more quickly and more surely to the perfection of charity.

We cannot expound here the sublime and subtle doctrine which establishes the lawfulness and excellence of the letter of the counsels. We can merely say that it is not because created things or creatures are bad that the Lord counsels their renunciation. It is because our hearts are not sufficiently pure. Catholic tradition has put forward some profound reason which can be reduced to the following headings: 1. The letter of the counsels witnesses to the transcendence of the love of God alone; 2. it proclaims the world to come, in which we shall be as the angels of heaven; 3. it preserves the peace and simplicity of our hearts; 4. it renders us wholly free for the preaching of the Kingdom.

It is therefore the *letter* of the counsels which distinguishes the religious vocation from that of the laity.

The laity are called to follow Christ in and through those great human realities, family love and a temporal profession. The way of the layman is through the reality and intensity of these great blessings. His vocation is to shoulder them courageously. His peril is to allow himself to become wrapped up in them. That is why, to be a saint, he has need of the spirit of the evangelical counsels. Then sanctity is open to him—it is for God that he takes up this way with courage and purity of heart. But religious are called to follow Christ directly, by renouncing those things which constitute the way of the layman. They renounce them, not because they are bad, but because the Lord is immeasurably greater, more grand, and because the heart, wounded by sin, runs the risk of distraction in possessing them. This renunciation through love then becomes a great witness to love, and their hearts are free. Sanctity is open to them; it can more easily be theirs. Their peril is simply that they may fail to give the intensity and earnestness to their love that their brethren in the world give to their wives and children.

One can go further. The charitable love to which laymen are called is a love which 'includes' those blessings which constitute the vocation to which mankind is called (conjugal love, etc). The charitable love to which religious are called is a love which excludes them. God alone, Christ alone, will be their only good. So the charity and hence the vocation of the religious is described not only by the word 'total', but also by the word 'exclusive'. All Christians are called by their baptism to sanctity—that is, to love God with all their heart, with all their soul, and with all their mind. A 'totality' is therefore demanded of them all; at very least they must be tending towards it. But this 'totality' of their heart for God by no means excludes, but rather includes, the bringing up of a family, and having a place in the city of men. On the other hand, the charity to which religious are called must not only gradually take possession of their whole heart, but must embrace God alone.

We come now to the great reality of consecration, to that 'portion' which God reserves for himself alone.

Here again, a theological study would show that the most radical consecration is effected at baptism. Just as the Hebrews were set apart from the pagan peoples around them by their vocation, and the sign of this consecration was circumcision, so the Christian people are set apart by God and consecrated to the one, crucified and glorified Lord, to whom they belong, and the sign of this consecration is the sign of the cross. No subsequent consecration attains such intensity. For in it the most secret place of the soul, its very essence, created and re-created, is 'called', in the fountain of living waters beneath the sign of God, the Trinity, and of Christ crucified.

But just as although the Hebrews as a whole were set apart, yet God chose individuals from among them and reserved them for his exclusive service, so from among the Christian people wholly set apart and consecrated, God picks out some more exclusively, and reserves them for himself, to proclaim still more illustriously that he is Lord above every name.

The call to the letter of the counsels possesses something in the nature of a seizing by God of certain individuals. They are more especially his portion. And the Church, faithful to the spirit of her Lord, is familiar with the institution of consecrated virgins and their solemn consecration. With their baptism at the heart of it, they are more particularly God's portion among the Christian people, belonging exclusively to him and his service.[1]

Finally, the specific object of the religious vocation could be defined in this way: with baptism at its heart, it is the call to follow Christ

---

[1] We can see why the word 'vocation' should not, strictly speaking, be applied to marriage; vocation really signifies a properly supernatural call from God. Such a call is not necessary before getting married—nature itself is sufficient for this. But for vowing one's whole life, one's consecrated virginity, to God, nature will not be sufficient. For that, a call from God is necessary, a 'vocation' in the proper sense of the word.

alone, to the very end, by the literal practice of the evangelical counsels; the call to belong only to him, his person and his work.

III   THE FORM OF THE RELIGIOUS VOCATION

To understand this doctrine we have to try to define the form peculiar to the religious vocation and to distinguish it from the form of the apostolic vocation (the priesthood). Then we must try to formulate the kind of grace related to this vocation, and where it is imprinted in the person called.

I mentioned above the two lines of 'development' within baptism—the 'belonging to God' and 'service'. We have placed the religious vocation in the first category, and the apostolic vocation (the priesthood) in the second.

In actual fact, of course, things are not quite so clear cut. Every vocation to belong to God includes also some kind of ministry and mission in the Church. Thus, nuns have received 'mission' to lift up the Church's praise to God. Similarly, 'being with God' is an essential of every ministry.

In our own day particularly the priestly conscience finds its stimulus to sanctity in its apostolic mission. Yet there are two distinct objects, and if, in practice, the Church associates them, they nevertheless remain distinct, and hence capable of giving rise to two distinct vocations. The priestly vocation is determined by a ministry; the religious vocation by the literal practice of the counsels.

This point stands out clearly when we realise that these two vocations take different forms. A religious vocation appears rather in the form of an interior call which is actually sanctioned and finally ratified by the Church; the priestly vocation is rather in the form of an hierarchical commission.

So the vocation to the religious life appears in the form of an interior call, and with it we are concerned with the order of sanctifying grace, and with an intimate and personal invitation to perfection. 'If thou wilt be perfect . . .' is introduced into the history of the soul's relationship with Christ. That is why the term 'call' seems to be more applicable than the term 'commission', and the word 'interior' better than the word 'hierarchical'. And that is why, if it is to be discerned, there must first of all, if we may so put it, be a careful 'auscultation' of the soul.

Undoubtedly the priestly vocation also includes an interior call to follow Christ. But if we examine it more closely, we shall see that this is not its distinctive form. Its specific and proper form is that of 'mission' and even of 'hierarchical mission': 'Go and preach'. A simple comparison between religious profession and ordination to the priesthood will be sufficient to elucidate these two forms. It is the postulant, moved by grace, who presents himself at the monastery door and begs the favour of admission to what is, as it were, the official School of the *Sequela Christi*. Again it is he who presents himself for profession. But where holy Orders are concerned, it is no longer the candidate who presents himself. It is the hierarchy of the Church which calls him. The candidate presents himself for profession, moved by an interior inspiration, but not for Orders—he is presented and called to them. There would seem to be a good illustration of what we are putting forward here—on the one hand an interior call, finally ratified by the Church; on the other, a commission by its hierarchy.

This difference perhaps also explains why, in a religious vocation, the place of rational deliberation and prudent judgment is more marked than in the ministerial vocation of the priesthood: 'If thou wilt be perfect', the Lord said. He proposes a way. He asks that it should be considered. He does not impose it. But vocation to the ministry is more imperative: 'Go and preach'. We ought, in practice, to exercise the same restraint. In the case of religious vocations it is in the last resort for the individual to decide for himself. Undoubtedly the Lord's invitation can be very pressing: 'Go, sell what thou hast'. However, the Lord proposes, but leaves men free: 'If thou wilt be perfect'. In the last resort it is up to the individual's own prudent judgment.

Can we now attempt to determine what precise part of the person is affected by this divine call to the religious life?

It affects the whole of being, body and soul. Even in the womb God fashions those who are truly called by him. But particularly it affects what we call the basic will,[1] by which we mean the root of the will, i.e. the positive desires of an individual and not simply the level of his thoughts. Vocation is not merely something on the intellectual level but is on a more vital plane, that of individual personality, history and end. Basic will also means the level of the will which is properly spiritual and free and not that pertaining to the instincts or sensible

---

[1] We are only concerned with basic will. The following chapters on the various criteria for judging vocations will deal with aptitudes.

appetites. Only at the 'basic' level is it possible to form strong and settled purposes which will endure throughout a man's whole life and only there divine grace finds its proper object. Finally, by this properly spiritual and free will we mean what is most stable, personal and true, that which grips the individual at the very core of his being. This basic will, then, expresses the very essence of the individual. The great thing is to isolate it and to be sure that we are really dealing with it, and not with some imagined will which sooner or later will betray itself. Normally, if we can really discover what a person wills in his innermost heart, we shall know what he was created for, and therefore what God is calling him to do. It often takes a long time, especially for the person concerned, to find out what is really willed.

This basic will is the fruit both of grace and freedom, but first and foremost of grace. Only God can form it; without God's call it is a purely human thing which sooner or later will fail. But the call from God which stirs up and envelops the will needs some response from man as well. Vocation can be compared to an acceptance which is formed by the action of grace and of freedom. Normally it has its own history; it may come at five or at thirty years old, it may develop slowly or be born almost instantaneously, it may be beset with doubts or certain from the beginning, it may encounter much opposition or know no strife at all. Whatever the circumstances, the question is always to discover whether the acceptance is genuine, formed in the depths of the soul by grace, or is simply a fabrication of the mind or a deceptive diversion of the appetites. In the case of the true vocation, we have a mature fruit springing from the depths of the being and of grace, and a wholehearted response to God—'Be it unto me according to thy word'. Here, the pleasure and purpose of God is that his creature should be his alone and live entirely for him and his service. 'If it is really God's purpose, the soul is able to give a "yes" so full and so unifying that it will endure and increase throughout this life.' This is what we mean by the grace of vocation in the basic will.

We have just described the grace of vocation. Is it possible to define more formally in what this grace consists? It pertains to the order of sanctifying grace, *gratum faciens*, and not merely to charismatic grace for the sole benefit of the body. It comes from God, who calls a creature through love to make him holy as a follower of his Son. Is it in the sphere of actual grace or habitual grace? In theory, it belongs to the sphere of actual grace. It is an illumination and a motion from God, which strikes into a man's life and shakes it to its foundations. Sometimes its coming can be actually dated, but as a rule, like life itself, it comes silently and almost unperceived.

But in so far as it expresses the decree of divine predestination, it also gives direction to the life in question and lasts as long as that life itself. So it does seem as though we must regard it as sanctifying grace itself, directed towards a definite end, and as definitely individualised to the particular person concerned. This seems quite clear in the case of vocation to the priesthood where there is a sacrament and an indelible character. The grace of the priestly vocation then passes into the character through the grace of the sacrament of Order, and impresses itself permanently and deeply upon the whole life of the priest. In the case of the simple religious vocation, there is neither sacrament nor character. Yet even this has its permanent element. There is, on the one hand, the call of God which, of its very nature, cannot be rescinded although it remains quite free. And on the other hand, there is the religious state itself. Vocation, when recognised by the Church by solemn vows, places the religious in a certain *state* of life which is more than a particular way of organising it; it is a disposing of the innermost personality which St Thomas coupled with consecration. Can we not say, then, that at this point vocation is combined with sanctifying grace so that it is orientated, one might say individualised, in a permanent way in the religious state? From this point of view the grace of vocation is rooted in a stable state of life which is, by its very nature, definitive. The religious is always able to call on it, and especially in moments of crisis.[1]

To sum up these ideas on the grace of vocation: we considered it first in the mystery of divine predestination, then in the grace of baptism, where it becomes manifest in a more particular call to follow Christ in the way of the counsels to the end, to be wholly and exclusively his. We recognise this grace with reverence when it blooms and flowers in a child, who, however confusedly, intends to live for God alone. And we greet it with equal respect in an old religious who, at the end of her life, brings to her Lord alone the offering of all her love.

FR B.-M. CHEVIGNARD, O.P.

---

[1] We are not concerned here with the important question raised by dispensation from solemn vows.

CHAPTER III

THE CRITERIA OF VOCATION—
THEOLOGICAL APPROACH

THE QUESTION of the signs, or of the manifestations of a religious vocation is vitally linked to the principles of revelation about the nature of the divine call, the subject of Fr Chevignard's masterly exposition in the previous chapter.

Our concern to find trustworthy criteria is bound up with the fruitfulness of those lives and institutions which are blessed with the flowering of true vocations; its importance is equally witnessed by the tragedy of so-called 'lost' vocations or of lives lived in religion without any vocation. Now the signs of a vocation are not only the gratuitous ones which can be categorised, like facial characteristics, signs which are the result of grace and human correspondence with it. But it is mature experience which will develop the initial presumption into positive certitude. If the priest often has to confirm this intial presumption then he will become more and more qualified to collaborate with aspirants, superiors and novice mistresses in the progressive developing of vocations and in helping them to achieve their effective fulfilment.

The following considerations are confined to vocations raised up through the ordinary channels of providence: I have deliberately excluded calls which come in the extraordinary form of charismatic favours. They are substantially valid for all vocations, both of men and women, but in applying them to the present-day situation as far as women are concerned we have to reckon with the need for critical justification. To this end, the pastoral task of the priest is less concerned with translating relevant doctrinal propositions into moving language or exhortation than with directing and integrating into a theological synthesis a too exclusively analytical reasoning.

The proper theological sources for our subject are first, canon law and secondly the living pastoral tradition. In theory these two authorities ought to be mutually complementary without confusion. But in practice they frequently use dissimilar terminology and, because they

ignore each other both are impoverished and fall short in their functions. Probably theology can furnish the necessary correctives both to a
too literal interpretation of the law and a too wordy empiricism in
spiritual direction, and such correction may increase both their
effectiveness and their favour with the faithful.

The indispensable signs of vocation required at the time of entry
into religion are a *right intention* and a *proper aptitude for the observances
and works of the particular institute* (can. 538).

Aptitudes or dispositions, to which most impediments can be traced,
are clearly less dependent on the human will than a right intention.
It will be easy to show the existence of some of them. In the case of
others, prudence will suggest recourse to the specialist. Although the
common law of the Church makes no mention of it, constitutions and
custom increasingly require a general and special medical examination.
In Chapter IV Father Beirnaert, S.J., puts the case for making use of
the latest scientific discoveries and explains the circumstances in which
they can help to understand the psychology of the individual candidate
for the religious life. There can be no doubt that, frequently, scientific
methods of investigation, applied by specialists, cast doubts on the
effectiveness of those empirical rules for the discerning of spirit which
are sanctioned by an approved tradition. In practice the fact that there
is interpenetration between all the vocational criteria means that the
question of the influence of the natural dispositions on the rightness of
the intention frequently arises. And here we enter the sphere of the
theologian.

The question of a right intention, as far as the external is concerned,
amounts to the absence of error or deceit. And because of the higher
interests of public order involved in a person's state of life, it is on this
right intention that the Church centres her canonical examination of
the individual candidate in the case of women's vocations.

But the negative criterion of a presumption on the border land
between the external and internal cannot possibly ignore the positive
factor of the divine appeal, perceptible only to the heart. Canon 541
bears this out by its manifest concern that the candidate should possess
a mature judgment and a committeed conscience, as regards his personal vocation, as a condition underlying his request to be admitted
into religion.

By linking the requirements necessary to satisfy the external conditions to the substance of those secret confidences he has received, the

priest will be able to open the aspirant's eyes to the depth and the riches of that right intention which is the test of the divine call. In the light of theology we can say that at the very heart of every vocation there is certainly a special 'revelation' to be reckoned with which is something quite distinct from the faithful adherence demanded of all believers and from the admiration common to the many to whom it has not, however, been given to perceive the pre-eminence of evangelical perfection.[1]

It will, then, be the theological interpretation of revelation which will make the priest as much an *awakener* of vocations, directing attention to the way of the counsels, as a judge whose decision is sought on the authenticity of that higher and interior call which is the mark of the incipient vocation.

Since the gifts of the Holy Spirit presuppose sanctifying grace, but not necessarily such a force that the practice of the moral virtues is compulsory, one of the most important signs of a vocation will be concern on the part of the candidate to preserve himself in a state of grace and to be humbly obedient to the promptings of the Spirit.

The choice of evangelical perfection in the form of a particular state of life associated with the visible structure of the Church must be made promptly, with the supernatural comprehension and generosity of divine grace.[2] For the consecration of one's whole life, which Pius XII states is the primary object of a religious vocation, is also the end from which the rightness of the intention and its warranty are derived. It is important, in applying the psychological doctrine assumed in theology,[3] to distinguish carefully the simplicity of this choice from the complications which arise from external circumstances when it is put into practical operation.[4]

Of course a particular institutional form of the religious state is frequently embodied in the vocation as such. But it does also happen that, failing inspired intuitions, a final decision may be brought about only by means of human effort in the practice of the moral virtues. Particularly in subjects blessed with several strings to their bow, or burdened with some relevant contrary-indication, the vocation to evangelical perfection itself must not be called in question simply

---

[1] cf *Summa Theol.* I–II, 68, 2: Pius XI, Encyc: *Rerum Ecclesiae*; A.A.S., 1926, p. 76: encyc: *Mens Nostra*; A.A.S., 1929, p. 701.
[2] *Summa Theol.* II–II, 189, 10.
[3] *Ibid*, I–II, 6.
[4] *Ibid*, 12.

because of hesitations about an active or contemplative form of life or its liturgical or penitential character, not to mention the new alternative between a religious or a secular institute which now adds to the difficulty of choosing between houses of the same observance or between congregations engaged in similar work.

On the other hand subjective certainty about the choice of the way of the counsels must submit any move towards a particular form of the religious life to the judgment of the hierarchy. For the quality of the individual vocation will depend, in large measure, on the extent to which circumstances and incidentals, in themselves indifferent and fortuitous, are assimilated into the simplicity of the essence of the vocation itself.[1] Purity of intention, in ascetic doctrine, is in actual fact inextricably bound up with its rightness.

Far from being capable of peremptory solution, this question of vocation continues after entry into religion. Its answer is to be sought in making the initial signs explicit and in particular by applying the intention to the second object, i.e. to the means employed to attain evangelical perfection.[2] This pre-eminently ascetic aspect of vocational signs is found in the programme for the novitiate sanctioned by canon law (can. 565). Rather than a trial run for the physical observance of the vows the novitiate ought to be the practical school for making the future religious into a virtuous person, capable of seeing the perfection of the counsels and their sanction in solemn vows in the light of virtue. Superogatory works, in fact, can only stem from virtue; they are vitally linked to it and they are, as it were, its flower and crown. And since this virtue, St Thomas says, is met with in but few men, I am inclined to think its acquisition is a more certain sign of vocation than outward conformity to the rule.

The criterion of this virtue, which issues from the depths of conscience and flows thence into outward conduct, will not so much be the actual practice of each and every one of the moral virtues, for the novitiate is hardly the field for exercising the majority of them, but rather the development of a quality common to them all—a certain integration, a simplicity of spirit and proportionate even-ness in the growth of the virtues.[3] The genuineness of these signs is evidenced in the interior spirit by theological charity and prudence which inform

[1] *Summa Theol.* I–II, 18.
[2] *Ibid.*
[3] *Ibid.* I–II, 64–66.

all the virtues. I must point out that the authenticity and generosity demanded by young people today seem to postulate here a theological formation in their teachers which is often wanting: at the same time they imply a compliment which goes much further than the actual dispositions of the candidates themselves.[1]

Although his strongest leanings—*proclivis inclinatio*—are the candidate's own secret, the practical manifestations, i.e. the habitual indications, of this intention relative to ends and means, provide superiors with a positive criterion for judging suitability for incorporation into the commumity by solemn profession (can. 571).

Finally, the evidence of the *religious* spirit (can. 647) in the professed, persisting in the life of the visible Church, is the final and authentic sign of that unseen divine initiative which is a vocation.[2] Only once does canon law use the expression which is familiar enough to spiritual authors. To ask theology to interpret it is not to betray it. To test the religious spirit is a proper function of the external forum. It is the exercise of a pastoral prudence based on supernatural principles, and equipped with the premises laid down by revelation, so that it can recognise the secret operations of grace, and direct and estimate the correspondence possible in a sinful man ransomed by Christ.

The priest whose duty it is to give pastoral help to religious is by that very fact appointed to exercise the ministry of a theologian commissioned by the hierarchy in which the *magisterium* itself is deposited. When it is a question of guiding consciences regarding the observance of a rule with which he himself is not necessarily familiar, of judging between different views, of enlightening doubts of novice mistresses, novices, superiors and inferiors, of every age, he must be prompted by theology, whose task it is to speak of the things of God in God's way.

FR JULES FOHL,
Monk of Clervaux.

---

[1] There is a diagnosis of right intention, in terms of Canon 565, in Pius XI's encyclical *Ad catholici sacerdotii*, A.A.S., 1936, p. 40.

[2] The Holy See has invariably refused to accept 'loss of vocation' as a ground for dispensation from vows. *S.C. Epp. et Reg.*, November 1866.

CHAPTER IV

THE CRITERIA OF VOCATION—
PSYCHOLOGICAL APPROACH

IN DISCERNING vocations experience teaches us the importance of keeping the psychological aspect in mind. Cases are by no means rare of religious who, after several years of religious life, show signs of becoming unbalanced, of outbreaks of depression, morbid and obsessive jealousy, inability to eat or sleep, fear of going out alone, an intense emotionalism sometimes accompanied by signs of homosexuality, an attitude of opposition which remains impervious to correction, suicidal tendencies, an overwhelming feeling of inferiority. Subjects of this kind are a burden on the community. They suffer themselves, and make those around them suffer too. They become incapable of fulfilling their religious obligations, and there is often the danger that they may cause scandal.

Such religious are not always devoid of spiritual worth. Often they make tremendous efforts to shake off their condition. But usual spiritual remedies and the ordinary methods of prevention and encouragement are not effective with a condition which appears to be governed by psychological factors.

There is no question of denying the power of grace, but we have to recognise what experience teaches us i.e. that grace, in the normal course of things, works no more miracles in the psychological order than in the physical order. So side by side with the bodily health required in a candidate for the religious life in a given congregation, mental health must also be taken into account.

The discernment of the psychological balance required for the religious life is quite distinct from the task of spiritual discernment which falls on the representative of the Church, and which has its own tests. It pertains to the director, in the last resort, to pronounce on the authenticity of the vocation. The psychologist can only give an opinion as to whether, from his point of view, there are or are not any negative pointers. His judgment is concerned with the psycho-

33

logical conditions necessary for the actual practice of the religious life, and not with the candidate's spiritual aptitudes as such.

He has to discern, not whether the individual is generous, pious or apostolic, but if he is psychologically capable, without developing psycho-pathological symptoms, of leading a life which on the one hand imposes a certain number of onerous obligations, and on the other can be the occasion of dangerous illusions.

Now the experiences of those religious mentioned at the beginning indicate that such a discrimination should have been possible at the time when they first presented themselves as candidates. The symptoms which appeared after some years of religious life did not spring up out of the blue; they were rooted in the individual's past history. An inability to face up to a situation, depression, opposition, and abnormal sexual reactions, are signs of underlying factors which were present long before the circumstance which made the trouble obvious. If the candidate was admitted it is either because attention was not paid to certain clear signs, or because their importance was not recognised.

On this general level the idea of a psychological appraisal raises no problems. But when we want to put it into practice, and ask ourselves how it is to be done, the difficulties begin. It is on this point that I should like to offer some suggestions.

First of all, is it necessary for all candidates to submit to examination by a psychiatrist or a competent specialist, just as they now have to have a medical examination?[1] I do not think so. Apart from the fact that such a provision would in fact be very difficult in practice (e.g. the specialists too remote and too few, the candidates reluctant, family or society opposed), novice mistresses, superiors and directors have usually a psychological perception which very quickly enables them to detect candidates about whom there is no doubt. Candidates whose progress throughout the school has been followed, or who have been seen at work for several years, especially when their history and family background are known, may very well be the object of a psychological assessment without any visit to a specialist. Some will be admitted without any difficulty, others as easily rejected.

----

[1] cf The *Monitum* of the Holy Office, 15.7.61. *Improbanda est opinio eorum qui* autumant praeviam institutionem psychoanalyticam omnio necessariam esse ad recipendos Ordines Sacros, vel proprie dicta psychoanalytica examina et invesitgationes subeunda esse candidatis Sacerdotii et Professionis Religiosae. Quaod valet etiam si agitur de exploranda aptitudine requisita ad sacerdotium vel religiosan grofessionem. Simliter sacerdotes et utriusque sexus Religiosi psychoanalystas ne adeant nis Ordinario suo gravi de causa permittente.

But there are a certain number of doubtful cases. They must be singled out so that they can be sent to the specialist. Here, attention must be paid to signs which, without being in themselves negative pointers, do justify, and even by virtue of prudence demand, a thorough psychological examination.

A great service would probably be rendered to all those concerned with discerning vocations if these alarm signals, which experience shows are often but the superficial symptoms of some deeper disorder, could be collected and listed for their benefit. Evidence of them would obviously be no substitute for that ingenuity of mind, and that sort of 'sense' which gives warning that all is not well with a certain individual, but it would be a notable help. Until such a work is forthcoming, here are a few useful pointers.

Failure in studies, difficulties in following a simple argument, puerile disingenuousness, may indicate mental weakness. Lack of frankness on the part of the candidate, especially when accompanied by a certain unsociability, always raises doubts. It may occur in the case of a divided personality or of a dreamer or, more simply, in a girl who has something to hide. Of course, the possibility that she will come to the point and open out is not excluded, and then she can be made aware of the insignificance of what she was hiding; but it is also possible that grave matters are involved, which have made a deep mark. Here, at any rate, we shall see that she is sent to the specialist who, even if he is unable to make her talk, will be able to detect the significance of her silence.

A general attitude of opposition, a want of judgment which renders her impervious to criticism even in apparent assent, can be signs of a paranoia, the development of which, in the religious life, can make subjects ungovernable.

Crises of depression, with or without migraine and insomnia, a constant feeling of inferiority, can lead, later on, to uselessness. The kindness and encouragement of superiors and companions are often completely ineffective in face of a condition which frequently has very deep roots.

Anomalies in sexual developments are also alarm signals which are not to be disregarded. Although it is clumsy to urge the individual to confidences she is clearly reticent to give, it is nevertheless important to pay heed to every symptom in this connection. A homosexual tendency, especially if it has passed into action, and if it is accompanied by an antipathy towards the opposite sex, cannot be considered unimportant. Nor can a sexual neutrality which might be associated with troubles in connection with the menstrual cycle, or persistent acts of compulsive masturbation, especially if they lead up to fantasies involving violent scenes with anyone. These disorders in sexual development are not to be confused with the relative facility with which some girls renounce marriage. They are usually accompanied by other symptoms: irritability, periods of depression, the need to disparage or shun men, etc.

An almost exclusive taste for suffering, an overpowering necessity to be identified with the most bereft, in a society different from that of one's origin, also raise problems, in so far as they are bound up with an inability to allow joy or to give oneself to all.

These are only a few of the signs it is as well to heed in discerning a vocation. They will not easily go unnoticed if a detailed account of the history of the vocation and a specific inquiry into family background have previously, as it were, given the alert.

He who is responsible for discerning the vocation ought not to hesitate to get the candidate to explain the origin of her vocation in detail, and all the circumstances surrounding its appearance. Such an account is often very revealing. Take this example. A young woman of twenty-six wished to enter a contemplative order. She had taken a job after leaving the secondary school, and had served in the women's auxiliary army. She was not on good terms with her own family, and had on several occasions to ask for shelter with a friendly family who had a boy and a girl about the same age as herself. In a moment of loneliness, she had guilty relations first with the girl, and then with the boy. She was disgusted, and took herself to task. Now the idea of her vocation first arose in the following circumstances. When she was ten she had joined the Guides, and had occasion to be present at Christmas Mass in a Trappist monastery when she was about fourteen. The thought of the white monks celebrating the Lord's birth made quite an impact on her: 'Could not I, myself, be like them in an order of women?' The idea of vocation had been sown, but in circumstances so singular as to call for a most searching inquiry. She was then asked if she had not previously experienced a feeling similar to that which had come over her at La Trappe. She promptly remembered that she had been fascinated by the sight of one of the ceremonies at the Sacré-Coeur de Montmartre when she was seven: 'The Blessed Sacrament, the lights, the sacred ministers, the crowd of choir boys with their censers . . .' At this point she began to blush, and said:

'When I was little, I had only one wish—to be a choir-boy, and have a censer myself. I even remember, when I was about four or five, I made a censer of my "very own", with a basket at the end of a piece of string. I hid it well, so that no one should see it, and I played with it unknown to anyone. When I was about ten I realised that I could never be a choir-boy because I was a girl and not a boy, and I was in despair for several days! It was then that I asked to join the Guides—yes, that was one way of being a little bit like boys. It is true that I have always wanted to be a boy.'

It was not hard to make this girl see that there was probably some connection between her former wish to be a choir-boy and her present desire to be a choir nun. She agreed, then, to reconsider her vocation and to start questioning herself again.

We can see how the circumstances in which a vocation was born can attract attention and arouse further questioning. It is quite obvious, in the case we have just mentioned, that the candidate's attitude, which she herself had revealed in her own life-story, demanded a more thorough investigation.

An inquiry into family background can likewise make for uneasiness on some points. It is very unusual for lack of harmony between parents, or their want of balance, or the early disappearance of one of them, not to have its effect on a person's psychological make-up. Similarly, there are girls who were not accepted by their mothers in childhood, others who arrived instead of the desired boy, yet others who have suffered greatly through having a more brilliant sister. . . . All this can be noted and borne in mind, especially if the person's actual behaviour does not seem to be quite normal.

It is not, we repeat, for the director of conscience to make a diagnosis, but simply to raise the question of a person's psychological aptitudes, and to call in specialist assistance.

The specialist will answer the question which has been asked, and only that. He will reply, either by stating what negative pointers were behind the candidate's desire to adopt the kind of life envisaged, or by reducing to their true significance those difficulties which had been the object of the consultation, and concluding that from his point of view he can see no obstacles. This latter eventuality is less rare than one might think.

The role of the specialist is a delicate one. It does happen, in fact, that superiors sometimes wish to shift the responsibility for informing the candidate that she was not made for their congregation on to him —for they have come to this conclusion before he has been consulted. I do not think that is a very good interpretation of the specialist's function. It is up to the congregation to shoulder its responsibilities after receiving the specialist's report, for, in the last resort, it is the congregation that accepts or rejects the candidate. Nor do I think that the specialist can be satisfied with playing the part of the expert towards the candidate. When she goes to see him and agrees to confide in him, in some way he takes charge of her to find out, with her co-operation, what is the best way of life for her, conformably with her psychological make-up. A human tie is formed which cannot be reduced to a mere professional relationship. It can, therefore, be bad for the candidate when the specialist is but a kind of examiner whose verdict is awaited with trepidation. The specialist, in fact, must help the person to ask herself questions about her true bent, and to solve them herself for her own good. More consideration ought to be given to this delicate situation, which can only be made even more painful when the specialist is asked to serve as the congregation's executioner!

But the psychological discernment, when carried out with the necessary delicacy and competence, must serve both the good of the Church, which seeks religious capable of discharging the obligations they have undertaken, and also of the subjects themselves, who have the right to live their lives as women and Christians without the grave danger of suffering and the emergence of pathological symptoms.

LOUIS BEIRNAERT, S.J.

CHAPTER V

THE ROLE OF THE PRIEST, FROM CALL TO POSTULANCY

IF IT is true that vocation is not a static thing, but that once the Divine Call has been recognised and accepted a dialogue of love begins, a dialogue which consists of fresh appeals from the Lord and cheerful responses from the spouse, perpetuating the initial response, then it is important that candidates for the religious life should be given some help between the time when their vocation first appears and their becoming postulants. We are here concerned more particularly with the part the priest can play in this connection.

METHOD FOLLOWED

I would have preferred to deal only with the religious and spiritual help which is properly the priest's function. But experience proves that candidates for the religious life ask many practical questions which the priest cannot in charity evade. Timid, or at least reserved, at this decisive moment in their lives, they often have to face alone this mysterious land of Religion which beckons them; they do not know in whom to confide, where to turn for enlightenment on those immediate and concrete problems posed by the regulations, before their vocation can be realised. Is this really to be regretted? For it is easy for the priest, with an opportunity such as this, to give the candidate a realistic view of the religious life, the angelic aspects of which ought not to be allowed to conceal the human elements.

So in order to avoid this account being above the problems raised during this period preceding entry into religion, I have attempted several 'soundings' in various types of religious order for women— contemplative, active, mixed—with a view to collecting from the young sisters or the mistresses of postulants some actual evidence of the difficulties they experienced from the awakening of their vocation to their becoming postulants. I have sifted almost fifty personal replies from individuals, together with information recapitulated or summarised by the mistresses, which seems to me a broad enough range. To

39

collect the evidence I drew up the following questionnaire which will serve as the basis of this report.

QUESTIONNAIRE

I. Did you at any time have any difficulty in deciding whether to choose the active or the contemplative life? Or which religious family to enter? How did you choose? Were you helped at all—if so how? By the advice of a priest, the light of a retreat? Through reading, films, contact with different religious congregations?

II. A. What particular problems of an objective kind did you have to face while waiting to become a postulant?

For example: Attitude towards the family—had you to warn them? When? Did you meet with help or hindrance? The question of the dowry, the trousseau? Attitude towards your professional circle? Towards your secular friendships, and worldly things? Towards the clergy, parochial activities? What advice would your past experience lead you to give on these points?

To what risks do you consider a vocation is particularly exposed during this period? How should they be faced—or avoided?

B. Did your entry into religion find you fully prepared for it?

Did you form a correct idea of the religious life before entering it? Did you feel any apprehensions which it would have been possible to dispel previously? Were there any difficulties of adaptation which could have been avoided by a better preparation?

How did you really think of this preparation before entering? In its physical, psychological, practical, spiritual and religious aspects?

On what particular points of their preparation should we concentrate, to make the beginnings of the religious life a little easier for the young people of today?

(N.B. It seemed better to phrase these questions in a personal way, since we are looking for perfect frankness. The replies can be framed so that the anonymity and secrecy of every conscience may be respected.)

I. We will assume that a vocation is awakened and discerned, normally at any rate, as a vocation to the religious life. The eventual choice between active and contemplative life, or between this or that religious congregation (first part of the questionnaire), remains first of all to be determined, and then to be decided, with the help of the priest.

II. The choice having been made, the special problems of preparation itself arise—objective problems, and subjective problems connected with the personal preparation of the candidate (second part of the questionnaire).

I may say that this inquiry, far from discounting my own experience, has simply borne it out in every point.

I THE CHOICE

1. DOES THE PRIEST IN FACT ENTER INTO IT?

Do not imagine that the priest is invariably consulted at this critically important juncture. An old novice mistress of an active congregation in the West Country told me that most of the fifty-odd young people she had known could hardly be said to have had a director. The majority had decided for themselves after making personal inquiries of one or more institutes. The Prioress of one Carmel wrote to say that only two out of exactly ten cases had been influenced by a priest. Must we attribute this in the first place to the independence of modern youth, and, in the second, to the lack of interest in religious vocations on the part of confessors?

2. IN WHAT RESPECTS IS THE PRIEST CRITICISED?

Although, in most communities, there was closer contact with the priest in the discernment and direction of their vocations (it reaches 65 per cent in a nursing congregation), my investigations showed that the priest is far from being above reproach.

What youthful vocations expect of him, first of all, is 'witness'. Hence this confession from a former 'Jociste', now professed in a mixed institute:

'I was helped, during my first retreat, by meeting a holy priest who put me into contact with Christ. For the first time I met the love of God, personified in him. . . . I could scarcely believe it, because I had made a God for myself in the likeness of Monsieur le Curé, a strict master who could see everything, especially evil, and who read your very thoughts. Had I been able to dispel this atmosphere of fear earlier, it would have been easier for me to respond confidently to the call of God.'

Then, the priest should know how to use the opportunity to win their confidence. A Carmelite reports:

'When I was fourteen, I resolved to speak to my confessor about my vocation. He encouraged me considerably. A week later he left for a different parish. What happened then might be a revelation to some priests.

For several months after his departure, my confessions became a torture— I was afraid to speak, and every time, after their exhortation, different priests would say: "Go in peace", without one word more. I cannot say how hard I prayed to find a director. At last, on New Year's Eve, I went into some confessional and was quite surprised to hear the priest asking me a question, a trifling question at that: "What do you wish for the New Year? Good health?" Seizing the opportunity while it was there, I replied spontaneously: "Oh no!

A greater love of God." My reply interested him, and in this way began a direction which was to last right up to my entry into Carmel . . .'

But it is important that the priest's encouragement should be given with due restraint, especially in an age when young people take offence at any interference with their liberty:

'My director', confides a novice in a congregation of nursing sisters, 'never mentioned vocation to the religious life, which would have put me off completely, I think, before I could have taken the first step myself, had he not indirectly prepared me for it by putting me in personal contact with God, by emphasising the role of the Spirit and by strengthening my spiritual life.'

These youthful susceptibilities, it must be noted, are as strong negatively as positively. A point that stands out in the replies I have received from nuns as well as active religious is their shocked surprise because priests who are chaplains of organisations, Guides, Catholic Action groups, dwell at great length on the vocation to marriage and how lovely it is, but pass over vocation to the religious life in silence. Witness these forceful words from a novice mistress:

'Here, all young people emphasise what a hiatus, what a deficiency there is; never, either in study circles, retreats, or other gatherings, did they hear the religious vocation spoken about, whereas there is an abundance of preaching about marriage, presented as the one ideal in which a woman can find complete fulfilment.

Consecrated Christian virginity must be preached, and presented not only in its negative aspect of total self-giving in union with God, but with all its fruits of spiritual motherhood, and therefore as capable of being, for a woman, a higher ideal even than Christian marriage (St Paul to the Corinthians), and of giving complete fulfilment.

Is not the teaching which thus presents Christian marriage as the highest ideal for a woman really a naturalistic way of looking at things? Whereas they should be seen in the light of the supernatural, and then we should teach, as Christ does in the Gospel, as does the Apostle, and the Church of all ages, that. for a woman, marriage is not the only way of developing her personality to the full.

Religious virginity constitutes a more perfect state, because "here the Spouse is Christ" (Tertullian), and also because, consecrated to God, it possesses value as a state.

Could not the attention of priests who are responsible for guiding young people be drawn to this reminder given by Pius XII (Allocution to Superiors General, 15th September, 1952):

"We really wish to direct our words to those priests, laymen, preachers, orators or writers who have not a word of approval or praise for Virginity dedicated to Christ; who, for some years now, despite the warnings of the Church, and contrary to her mind, have conceded to marriage a fundamental superiority over virginity; who go even so far as to present it as the only means capable of ensuring the development and natural fulfilment of human personality: let those who speak and write in this vein give heed to their responsibility before God and the Church.... They must be numbered among those principles which are to blame for an issue which we can only speak of with sadness ... the insufficiency of vocations in all fields."'

I thought it would be a good thing to quote this long testimony, since priests may find it instructive on how to present religious vocation to the young, as a consecration of their whole being to the Lord, and especially of the heart with its power of love. It is also instructive about the attitude of those priests who dissuade girls from accepting the religious vocation, who speak of it as abnormal, not adapted to modern life, or who tirelessly delay the entry of their militants, whom they judge to be indispensable!

I observe the same severity towards religious institutes which are lacking in witness (bitter memories of a school which killed any desire to join that community, for example), or true disinterestedness, by thoughtlessly accepting candidates or by unwise attempts at recruitment.

'I asked my confessor', wrote a young sister in an active congregation, 'to write to a certain institute for information. The ardent letter sent by the superior, who received me with open arms, and said what a joy it would be to have me as a postulant, rather damped my enthusiasm: how could she accept me without knowing me? I didn't follow it up.'

3. THE PRIEST'S HELP IN MAKING THE CHOICE

Still, the priest is frequently asked—this is admitted by all—to help candidates to choose between the contemplative and the active life, or between this or that religious family.

The fundamental choice between the contemplative or the active life does not appear to be the most difficult to make. Our inquiry reveals that in the majority of cases, young people have a clear perception of the attraction of a particular way of life. Their aptitude for it needs to be confirmed. Indeed, it frequently happens, especially with contemplatives, that the attraction of the religious life and its precise 'bias' were perceived at the same time. One Carmel discloses a proportion of nine out of ten cases—the highest I have met—having opted without hesitation for that Order. On the other hand, it is not unusual for some development to take place in candidates destined for the active or mixed life. In the case of the former, the desire for a deep spiritual life had initially drawn them so strongly towards the contemplative life that they were momentarily deceived, both about their own aptitudes and the call to a direct apostolate (missions, teaching, care of the sick, devotion to the poor and the labouring classes). In the case of 'mixed' vocations, some of them only discovered the importance of prayer and the primacy of the spiritual through the apostolate; this experience was necessary to influence them in the direction of a mixed institute, or a predominantly contemplative one.

This means that for the purposes of discernment it is not superfluous to resort to the usual tests in regard to aptitudes. Contemplative vocations are stamped with the character of utter ferocity, they desire 'God first and God alone' (the phrase is to be taken broadly, and does not exclude a sense of the Church and of souls), they are drawn by praise or penitence, they are the 'transcendent' vocations. So far as aptitudes are concerned, because of enclosure they require the highest degree of nervous stability, a large share of good sense, and also bodily health to stand up to the fasts and austerities. On the negative side, it is as well to be sure that the candidate is not seeking to escape from this age because she is afraid of its responsibilities or of life generally. On any assumption, the investigation into aptitudes should be very broadly based, surveying the whole personality of the candidate physically, psychologically, intellectually, spiritually, and even her family background and present activities.

Let us add that this inquiry should be positive (the candidate's talents and qualities) as well as negative (her limitations and failings). After such an investigation the motives and inspiration behind the vocation —if it exists—will be more clearly identified.

It must not be thought that candidates for the active life are opting for an inferior spiritual life. They must possess an authentic fervour grounded on a zeal for souls, longing to express itself in the different works of the various religious families or institutes. A bold character and particularly good health are required in missionaries, intellectual qualities are imperative in teachers, etc. But this brings us to the second choice: between this or that religious family.

This choice often proves more difficult than the first because of the particularly large number of active congregations and the imperfect knowledge which candidates have of them. The young are often almost incapable of recognising the congregation which suits them best. Both the particular activity which attracts them and the spiritual calibre of their souls must be taken into account. But frequently, to facilitate recruitment, so they imagine, many congregations have broadened their special fields of activity so far that specialisation is often lost sight of, and they do not all possess a well defined spirituality. The priest must have a good deal of perspicacity and shrewdness if he is to assist in the choice.

It is a fact that not all young people are attracted to congregations they are acquainted with through their activities or studies, as we have noted previously, although this is so in a certain number of cases.

It is desirable, in the first place, that the director should be in a position to present the inquirer with a sufficiently wide range of congregations. If he cannot know them all personally, at least he will have books and pamphlets about them at his disposal. But of course—all the replies bear this out—nothing can take the place of direct contact with these institutes. The ideal presented is sometimes far removed from the actual conditions in which it is realised. However, a retreat, some days of recollection under the wing of a community, are often the best way for young people to discover whether they feel at home in it.

Candidates, mistakenly, do not always bother to acquaint themselves with the various types of religious life before making their minds up. 'I am coming to see you in obedience to my director', a girl wrote to the superior of a congregation, 'but I have no desire at all to belong to your Order—I want to be a Little Sister of Père de Foucauld!' But let the confessor respect the candidate's calling, without trying to push his own preference for this or that congregation.

After making contact with the community, the candidate must be advised unequivocally that she must come to no final decision without some period of recollection. Nothing can take the place of the testing of time, together with prayer. The reading suggested by the superior or community chaplain, or possibly by her director, will complete the candidate's information.

It does not appear from the survey that films played an essential part in the choice, especially for contemplatives, only one of whom mentions L'Appel du Silence and another, negatively, Les Anges du péché. On the other hand, the actives attribute more importance to them. Monsieur Vincent comes first on the list, being mentioned by several, The Song of Bernadette only by one; several missionary films are also noted. We are often told that films about a community's daily life, or a presentation of its activities, are very desirable to enlighten vocations, but what often emerges from these documentaries as a whole is their all too obvious anxiety to stimulate recruitment. The young prefer a living witness.

Finally, in bringing this first section to a close, I must say that the priest would do well, once the choice has been determined, to recommend straight away a visit to a doctor who knows and esteems the religious way of life, for should a serious impediment be discovered it would be pointless to allow the candidate to entertain hopes which could not be realised.

II Preparation Proper

All are agreed that the priest has a very great part to play in this. He has to sustain the candidate by his guidance. These days, more than in the past, candidates expect the priest to possess understanding and sympathy, which, generally speaking, they cannot find in their own environment during this time of waiting.

A. Objective Problems

Before speaking about the candidate's personal preparation, we must consider a certain number of objective problems which most candidates have to face between the awakening of their vocation and their entry into religion. Although clearly of secondary importance, they raise very real difficulties for candidates who scarcely know in whom to confide at this time, and who, in the excitement of coming to a decision which will revolutionise their lives, feel the need for authoritative counsel. The survey reveals profound gratitude for directors who have been so bold as to make a stand, and who have prescribed a clear and prudent line of action, marked by disinterestedness and the spirit of faith, with regard to these problems.

1. The family: how and when should it be informed?

'The first piece of advice given me by my director, which, I might say, helped me very much', writes a former Jociste, 'was that I should not disclose my plans to anyone at all, not even to my immediate family circle, at least for some months. The soul needs tranquillity to experience the presence of God, to become aware of his call, and it is only when it has decided to respond to it that it is able to face up to objections of every kind . . .'

Although it would seem wise not to raise the question in the immediate family circle before a definite choice has been made and the candidate is sure about her vocation, nevertheless there should be no undue delay in breaking the news to them, especially if the family is a Christian one; experience shows that those who leave it until the last moment to tell their parents are certain to cause them distress, especially where they announce their vocation to the religious life and the rapidly approaching date of their entry both at the same time. The family needs time to get used to the idea, and does not like to be taken by surprise and confronted with an accomplished fact. It is suggested that they should be informed four, six, or at the most, twelve months before entry. Usually the candidate feels extremely relieved once the announcement has been made, for many young people are very worried, and some in great distress, at the thought of the possible reaction on the part of the family, especially of the suffering their departure will cause (particularly in the case of an only daughter, a father a widower, or an old and sick mother). It is for the priest to remind them then of the calls in the Gospel: 'He that loveth father or mother more than me is not worthy of me. . . . No man putting his hand to the plough and looking back. . . . And everyone that hath left house or brethren or sisters or father or mother or wife or children or lands for my name's sake, shall receive an hundredfold and shall possess life everlasting'. These divine words will strengthen the candidate and enable her to face suffering, especially that which she is going to inflict on loved ones. For it is clear that even the most faithful families, where parents are delighted that God has been pleased to call one of their children, do not find it easy to overcome their feelings. The sacrifice is no less felt for being generously offered.

This is one reason why the announcement ought not to be made too soon, so that the pain is not intensified by a prolonged period of waiting, nor yet too late to allow time to alleviate it before the departure. The ideal would be for the family to guess the truth bit by bit, for them to have a somewhat confused presentiment of the transformations at work in their daughter's soul and demeanour. In any case, although vocation is a personal matter there is more to it than that, because it also constitutes a challenge to the faith and generosity of one's friends and especially one's family. It is then that mothers can appreciate what Mary's station at the foot of the Cross means, and that the repercussions of our actions are felt throughout the whole of the mystical Body: 'a soul which is exalted exalts the world'.

A novice puts the matter rather well when she recalls this memory:

'Vocation is a call from God; that being so, who was asking this sacrifice of mother (she was a widow), if not he? And was not the question really to inquire whether I had the right to doubt mother's generosity, and to refuse her this opportunity of growing in stature?'

It is not that the candidate receives any effective help, in many cases, from her own family.

'Even in a deeply Christian family', writes a novice, 'I have to admit that I found very little understanding; on the contrary, my father was so prostrate with emotion during the four months preceding my departure that he did not speak a word to me, or only opened his mouth to say that my departure reminded him of mother's death (yet father had remarried, led a normal home life, and I was not living with him). I met with difficulties from my sister, whom I had often helped with her children, and who did not approve.'

Even though the atmosphere may not be so depressing as this, one has often to refrain from any further reference to the impending departure, though silence is but the lesser evil. One is fortunate if there are no attempts to discourage the vocation, even in supposedly Christian families—the tragi-comedy of affection, proposals for exciting travels or introductions to suitors, objections and criticisms of all kinds (a too independent character, inadequate health). In this war of nerves, which is certainly useful in confirming the vocation, the priest's intelligent and resolute encouragement is invaluable; he can lift the candidate above these contingencies to the things of God and his appeal on behalf of love, the Church and souls sick for redemption.

When a girl foresees violent hostility on the part of her family to her vocation, it seems that it may be preferable to delay the announcement until the latest possible moment, to avoid painful and useless conflicts. There are actually some young people who, having broken the news, are careful not to give a definite date for their departure, and just quietly disappear. Usually things turn out all right in the end, but it sometimes takes a year or two. This is the time for remembering that 'we ought to obey God rather then men'. There is a severe testing, nevertheless, for the vocation which has unhappy memories of leaving home, and goes without news of the family. In such circumstances candidates are properly advised not to leave home before they are of age, and it is as well if they do not disclose the name of the priest who has helped them, to avoid tiresome and inopportune explanations.

Let the priest in return—indeed, in any case—be very discreet about any requests for information which are made to him.

A mistress of novices writes:

'One must be able to count on the absolute discretion of the clergy, when superiors get in touch with them for information about the families of girls who are coming forward. A case of grave indiscretion, which was extremely embarrassing for the candidate, has been brought to my notice.'

During the weeks preceding their departure, young people ought not to shun the affection of their families in order to make the separation easier. They ought rather to show them that their preferential love for the Well-Beloved who is calling them does not stifle the feelings and gratitude of their hearts. They will remain even more attached to their families than if they had left them to set up a new home. But they should always retain sufficient liberty to be able to avoid those late night sessions which might deprive them of Mass in the morning.

So far as distant relatives are concerned, all are agreed that the news of a vocation should not be broken until the last month, perhaps on the occasion of a farewell visit. Thus much pointless tittle-tattle and many indiscretions are avoided, and the candidate preserves her complete freedom of action to the very end.

It is for the priest to judge whether, in certain cases, there are any reasons for renouncing vocation or for delaying entry into religion (bereavement or sickness which necessitates the girl's presence at home; in large families there is often real need, for the time being at any rate, of the help which the older ones give, etc.). Finally, in those rare cases where the parents might seek to exercise pressure on one of their children to enter religion, it is the priest's duty to enlighten and liberate the candidate by making her perceive the real motives prompting her to remain faithful to her vocation—if they exist—and if they do not, then he should urge her to withdraw.

2. Dowry and Trousseau

Usually the dowry presents no great problem, and the candidate ought not to be daunted by it. Congregations, as a rule, are reassuring about this question, and their discretion is appreciated. Candidates and their families mostly respond by doing their very best. In the case of a poor girl, it is a good thing for the priest to broach the subject first, to emphasise that it is of secondary importance, and to suggest ways in which she might make at any rate some contribution (e.g. by putting something aside out of her wages against this eventuality, during the last year, or by appealing to a friend or benefactress). A former Jociste writes:

'It is important, among the working class, to make it clear that the religious life is not the preserve of a certain élite, necessitating, as a matter of obligation, a large dowry, which can be a considerable difficulty for many, intellectual attainments above the average, etc. The call of God has no need of these material values. But what he does want is a generous soul firmly resolved to refuse him nothing.'

On the other hand, families in comfortable circumstances should be made aware of the needs of religious communities, and ought to help them, as their own families, with true disinterestedness.

It appears from the survey that the question of the trousseau is a more delicate one—certainly in the eyes of a modern girl who is worried at the thought of clothing which, to say the least, is unusual. 'One is a little irritated', we are told, 'at the thought of wearing an outfit which is so different from that of the world, and little things like umbrellas and slippers put you in the wrong camp!'

Certainly in the eyes of the family too, in some cases. Of course, some of them like to prepare it for their daughter, but others lack either the time or the money.

Several young people worked to be able to buy it; others got it together themselves at less cost; yet others, in order to have freedom of mind, left the matter in the hands of a few religious. It appears that the priest would do well to advise the candidate to speak simply and frankly about it to the community she is to enter, and to see what will be best, thus avoiding any unwarranted anxiety.

3. Professional Colleagues

When the management is going to have no difficulty in filling the vacancy, and in any case so far as one's colleagues are concerned, the news should only be broken when one is actually about to leave. By far the best solution, where it is possible, is for the candidate to ask her employers to keep her job open, so that she can be reinstated should she prove unsuitable for the religious life.

A young religious sums up, in this assuredly happy formula, what the candidate's attitude should be: 'Say nothing, be "chic" and natural, and, on leaving, announce your vocation'. As a rule, the news causes a sensation and provokes thought, if not respect. Occasionally, however, candidates have to put up with distressing remarks: 'You have been disappointed in love. Are you afraid of life? Who ever suggested this desperate course to you?' The priest may then encourage the young lady to pray more and more for this world, which, together with its faith, has lost its sense of God.

4. Personal Relationships and Worldly Pleasures

Social functions, surprise parties, dances . . . there is, of course, no question of plunging headlong into these things by way of compensation to nature, anxious to enjoy itself to the full before the farewell, or of indulging in distractions to the extent of losing vocation. But the question which girls may ask the priest is whether they are allowed to maintain the outward pattern of their diversions, or if it is better to cut them all out altogether, so that they may thenceforth belong entirely to the Lord and so begin at once their preparation for the life of the convent.

Novice mistresses and young religious are, for the most part, agreed that there should be no sharp break, which might cause surprise, but that the candidate should act with a simple and natural circumspection, which will permit her to maintain her friendships and to go out when it is necessary, but will avoid any strain on her health and the risk of yielding to temptation, and which will make it possible for her to have a spiritual life, flexible, certainly, but adequate. There is very little spare time, anyway, when one has a job, and obligations to family and religious activities as well. Everyone declares that the candidate must be wholly occupied with the duties of her present state of life, and she must not want to copy in advance, and out of its proper context, the religious or monastic life.

It appears, however, that among the rising generation, less moderate considerations and attitudes are to be detected.

Accustomed to complete identification with and incarnation in her own environment, anxious to bear witness to the full, the religious is, up to the time of departure, quite an ordinary girl, who knows what she is leaving and what she is giving up; and there are those young people—even future nuns—who are almost shocked at the advice given above. I am told that: 'So-and-so made the most of life's pleasures right up to the last minute—the cinema, dances, sport, music, even visiting her good friends of the opposite sex to discuss serious social and religious questions and the problems of life'. This is a good thing in the eyes of modern youth, brought up to express itself and to be very understanding of what is natural and apparently genuine, but less ready to accept self-denial and that spirit of faith which will deepen them during their novitiate. There is something worth preserving in this desire not to offer to the Lord a personality which has been foolishly impoverished and truncated—the world is too apt to think that convents are peopled with the frustrated and those who have been left on the shelf—but it would be a serious matter if we were to forget original sin, and to think that we can place our unreserved confidence in nature. This is a sign of the times: formerly nature was often given insufficient recognition, for it is not fundamentally evil, but merely impaired. Today we have reacted against this idea so far as to forget the wound inflicted by original sin . . . perhaps this calls for some examination of conscience on our part as to the tenor of our preaching.

5. The Clergy and Parochial Activities

All agree that the parish priest, curate or chaplain must be warned in good time, but—forgive my referring to this again—there is evidence that many of them have an inadequate esteem and understanding of the religious life, and especially the contemplative life.

It is no slight trial for a vocation to find itself opposed by those who ought to be the salt of the earth.

The clergy must be advised, however, that it will be necessary to find a substitute to take over from the aspirant, who was perhaps in charge of Catholic Action or Guides, or held some other responsible position of leadership in the parish. Here again, we are told, the priest is often tempted to detain the aspirant, or to delay her entry into religion. A novice writes:

'Personally, I was helped very much by the example of a priest who was the father and inspiration of numerous activities, but who never put any obstacle in the way of a vocation or a personal aspiration, and who just accepted it that things would fall through as a result of so-and-so's departure, and that everything would have to be begun again. One really felt that he was doing God's work and not his own.'

In passing, I may say that it is desirable for this disinterestedness to continue after entry into religion. Although at the beginning, the role of the director may be useful in helping the new postulant to adjust herself, there is rarely any point in perpetuating these contacts at any rate as a normal thing. The pattern of life has changed, and its problems with it, and as a rule a girl will find more appropriate help in her new environment without any fear of tension between directives which may well be divergent.

Although there are cases where the director must see that the girl does not allow herself to be drawn into or distracted by too much activity, there are others where the priest—let us not be afraid to say so—will do the candidate a service by urging her into apostolic activity, as a support for her vocation during a prolonged period of waiting (a young professed nun declares how much help she received from a parochial guild at this time), as a test of balance, and as a challenge to confidence for a vocation naturally more attracted to silence and retreat.

'My director plunged me into Catholic Action, as a means of training me for the religious life. Since I was a teacher in a vocational school, this might have been too much! But no! Indeed, I became a YCW leader and then a Jociste president. Activity was really repugnant to me, yet I was very successful, they say. I learnt that it was by no means necessary to have led a cloistered life in the world to succeed in an enclosed Order. In the world, where activity is a duty, when the soul has a repugnance to activity it will complain bitterly about having no time for prayer, it will suffer because it has to adopt indirect means of leading people to God, it will very often have the impression that it is wasting time, yet all this, whatever we think about it, is a powerful force in deepening a contemplative vocation.'

The evidence marshalled in *Risquer sa vie pour Dieu* shows clearly that Catholic Action is an excellent school for vocations. But it is nevertheless true that young people trained by its methods have often more difficulty than formerly in entering straight into silence, recollection and contemplative retreat.

6. Risks run

We have already noted a few of these, from the temptation of a soft and comfortable life, which is liable to blunt one's generosity and ardour, to the strain (whatever the cause—work, apostolate . . .) which, coupled with the tension of leaving and the breaks which must be accepted, can occasionally be a threat to health.

In an attempt to correlate these external threats, I have related them to three interior defects which it is the director's task to detect and remedy:

(i) A subtle form of pride which tends to make one think oneself indispensable, irreplaceable. A former Jociste writes:

'A danger to which you can easily succumb, when everything conspires to give you this false impression. A danger which is met with not only if you are doing work of a professional character, but in the apostolate of Catholic Action. It is very difficult to be deeply attached to it, and at the same time to be sufficiently "detached" in your heart to be able to abandon easily an activity which has gripped you completely.'

Friends are naturally given to flattering this pride by voicing many thoughts and specious arguments which may impress the youthful vocation: 'Look how well you are doing as an actionist; who is going to take your place?' 'You are a social worker, a nurse; don't you think your secular life is just as useful and devoted?' 'How are you going to reach ordinary people, if you become a sister?'

(ii) A will which has not been sufficiently strengthened, and which is easily shaken by objections, afraid of what 'people will say', and of all the criticisms disseminated about convent life, which is gradually being overtaken by the temptations of the age.

'Temptations of all sorts', states one reply, 'doubts, discouragement, distress, subtle suggestions insinuating themselves into your mind. Is it not my duty to stay at home and help my family? (Because one is going to leave it, life with the family is more appreciated. All around, new families are springing up— one feels "alone".) Could I be mistaken, am I not choosing an easy life? [sic!] Should I not have more to fight for, should I not be more useful in Catholic Action? Am I going to become a mean and withered creature?'

(iii) A faith insufficiently awakened, badly instructed on the life of prayer and its primacy, and on the experiences of the spiritual journey, which can so easily be disconcerting!

'The more so', we are told, 'when you are endlessly running up against purely human reactions, and when you suffer terribly because you happen to be a sensitive person. Then you no longer see things clearly, and there is a grave risk of losing a true conception of values, your sense of vocation, and the reason for your departure.'

It is suggested, as a means of mitigating these dangers, that the period of waiting before entry could be shortened, but the importance of spiritual direction, contact with the community of one's choice, the necessity of prayer and communion, the benefit of serious reading, retreats and days of recollection, are given particular emphasis. This now brings us to the question of the candidate's personal preparation.

B. THE QUESTION OF THE CANDIDATE'S PERSONAL PREPARATION

1. Is preparation necessary?

Here we are certainly faced with a problem; this preparation, if it is desirable, is at any rate a delicate matter. In the majority of replies to my questions, young sisters are agreed that they had not formed an accurate mental picture of the religious life, and even add that it is impossible to do so before living it. Perhaps we ought to qualify this point of view by distinguishing the spirit of the religious life which can be foreseen, from its actual realisation 'in the flesh', as it were, in a multitude of observances which the candidate will discover through experience.

A prioress rightly observes how dangerous to a vocation a too carefully worked out idea of the religious life can be—let us leave this to the foundresses!—for with such a detailed picture in mind the candidate will have great difficulty in adapating herself to the rule she has chosen, and which she will profess. 'Mother, I am sorry that you do not have more adoration of the Blessed Sacrament here. I don't really like making my prayer in common . . . etc.' In this sense, it can be said to be fatal to enter the convent too well prepared.

'On the other hand', writes one who has taken temporary vows, 'it is important to enter the religious life with a great desire for re-birth and for fresh beginnings, and with a belief that one simply does not know all the paths which it will be possible to follow.' The most courteous thing is surely to be as malleable as wax, or as ready as a blank page on which the Lord may pen his loving purpose. The Gospel states: 'No man putteth new wine into old bottles'. How sound, then, was this advice given by a priest to a Jociste before she entered the convent:

'Forget everything you have learnt up to now, forget what you were, and your own little personal experience. Not that it will all be destroyed, but it is only when you have forgotten it that it will spring up again at the right moment, enriched with all that the religious life has taught you. Make yourself a new soul, utterly open to the grace of God, and forthwith put your whole trust in the religious family which has accepted you.'

This disposition of soul, which it behoves the candidate to acquire, does not absolve the priest from giving more detailed instruction on the 'enclosed garden' which religious life is, in the eyes of the people. A former Jociste says: 'It was a real mystery to me. My director, although a religious himself, did not consider it timely to lift the veil; I have often regretted it since.'

2. Fears and prejudices to be dispelled

First of all, on the negative side, the fears and prejudices which it would be good to dispel, since—I am told by a Benedictine friend—

the sufferings of the religious life are not, as a rule, what one imagined and feared they would be before one's departure.

I shall pass quickly over the exaggerations frequently repeated in the world, to which certain legends in the Breviary might lend colour.

'I thought', confides a young religious, 'that terrible corporal mortifications and external humiliation awaited me—which, to be sure, were not disclosed to the outsider—and that it went without saying that a religious took almost no food and slept on the floor. Although it was a little difficult for me at first not to have the satisfaction of such asceticism, which I could not actually have borne for very long, it became clear to me that the mortification of the will is always the more costly, and that humiliations come of themselves, indicating ever fresh failures.'

It is a fact that novices, even in the strictest orders, are at first scanda-lised by a way of life which to them seems to be too easy. But as a rule, within six months they have changed their minds and are even crying for mercy!

I think it is more profitable to pinpoint the prejudices of the young people of today, reflecting, as they do, the modern mentality. Here are the principal ones as revealed by the survey (it is clear that the priest will not have to intervene on all these points—that will depend on the candidate—but he should be as familiar as possible with them, so that he may act when necessary):

(i) The religious habit is unrealistic. It is deemed to be unhealthy, inconvenient for work, especially in a life of active apostolate, calcu-lated to lessen their influence, since it cuts them off from their surroundings and distinguishes them from other people.

'But we must also weigh its advantages', says a young religious. 'It creates a shock, and compels people to adopt a definite position. Setting the wearer apart for God, it awakens a sense of the holy. For we religious who care for people in their own homes, and are mingling with the masses, it is a protection which we have really felt at times!'

The Sovereign Pontiff, moreover, has given his verdict on the question, in the direction of moderate adaptation, by commending a simplification of dress in the immediate future.

(ii) Formalism of customs and terminology.

'The various points of ceremonial', confesses a former Jociste, 'and the formulae in use made my hair stand on end. Penances in particular appeared to me to resemble old fashioned and useless customs. It seemed quite clear that my chaplains and friends could hardly approve such anomalies. Our Jocist training created a duty, and that was to react against anything abnormal, even at the cost of our tranquillity. This somewhat assertive attitude was not calculated to facilitate the beginning of our postulancy. But imperceptibly I came to understand the meaning of these "religious" forms; if I had been instructed before entering, how much time would have been saved for more spiritual and balanced thoughts.'

Certainly there is no question of defending all the customs, nor of excusing all the expressions—why do we not return to a greater simplicity?—but at least their secondary character can be emphasised, so that essential things do not get buried beneath them. It is up to those responsible intelligently and prudently to be on the watch for adaptations rendered necessary by the present age.

'For the Church ought to bear in mind the temporal context whence her "chosen" have freely come, and young people must be helped to overcome that phobia of not being up-to-date. The stupidity of those who, wanting to be linked to the past, try to disguise and patch up old things to give them the appearance of new, is only equalled by the stupidity of those who, wanting to make innovations, begin by peremptorily effecting a clean sweep of the past. Beneath the seductive appearance of new values, and the obsolete aspect of the old, what is significant is their eternal constancy. Young people must be taught to recognise the true struggle against the stagnation resulting from an obsession with the past.'

(iii) The cloister is a barrier against worldly suffering.

They are afraid of being cut off from other people (v.s.—on dress), of no longer understanding them, and of losing their influence. It is suggested that: 'Perhaps this temptation springs from the modern attitude of mind which puts the salvation of souls before the glory of God'.

The cloister is by no means an 'ivory tower', and many people in the world are struck by the breadth of view possessed by contemplatives, by their awareness of the problems and needs of the contemporary world. He who holds unceasing converse with God owes it to himself to see and judge things as he does, from above!

(iv) The pettiness of the cloistered or common life.

'I was present at recreation with the postulants before entering, when the subject under discussion was refectory service. The least little things took on an exaggerated importance. When one has led an active life, and been saddled with responsibilities, these contacts make the details of community life, taken out of their context, appear petty and puerile.'

Or again:

'I confess that my service was very much hindered by certain religious who lacked any deep religious sense, criticised each other in front of the probationers, made use of the latter for despatching letters or keeping up particular friendships with other sisters. Want of vocational conscience, and want of probity and uprightness (there were certain religious, for example, who for several months received assistance to which they were not entitled, on the pretext that robbing the State is not stealing!).'

Far from regretting it, it is good for young people before entering to have personal experience of the limitations of human nature, even in the consecrated. This will avoid the temptation of scandal, later in the novitiate, on seeing the discrepancy between the ideal which they have of the religious life and the possible mediocrity of certain expressions of it, which they observe. This will be an incentive to them. The priest, without labouring the point, will have an interest in not hiding these unfortunate cases, but will recall the mystery of the Church which is human and divine, and of which both Priesthood and Communities are members.

(v) The Pharisaism of religious poverty.

'Youth', writes a sister, 'has an arbitrary and somewhat idealistic conception of poverty. The habits of camping, sport, mountaineering, have given them a taste for privations and the simple life.'

They would like to find this on entering the convent, and the simplicity of external forms in the recently established Congregations is a great attraction. They find it rather difficult to discover the poverty beneath the more conventional outward appearances of the old Orders, and this creates some real problems (e.g. a cell for one religious, which is big enough to house a whole family!).

Explain to them all the aspects of religious poverty. Our wretched age is touched by evidence of such penury, compared with which traditional poverty bears the appearance of riches. But how can we demolish what exists—chapels, cloisters—which would be very expensive to rebuild, even miserably?

Teach them the theological significance of poverty—liberation for God. And emphasise the mortification implied in the possession of things in common . . . and the intensification of work inside the cloister, which is the contemporary form of poverty. In this respect it would be as well to point out that poverty is not opposed to progress, to the purchase of machines, for example, which are necessary for productivity.

(vi) Obedience, an obstacle to the development of personality.

A horror of infantilism, an anxiety to be grown-up, and to be themselves. A fear of losing their personality through having to demean themselves by a robot-like obedience.

Point out the social significance of obedience (serving the common good), and its mystical aspects (the concrete expression of our faith; the submission to God in our superiors). The free immolation of our will makes us masters of ourselves, by liberating us from the old man and by bringing us into the liberty of the children of God. Can there be any doubt about the personality of the saints?

(vii) Equivocal attitude on renunciation.

'They are thought to be virile', says a former Jociste, 'because they sleep on bare boards, and happen to have accepted a way which will demand a physical effort, though this is done joyfully. In actual fact, they have to transcend all this, for it must give way to a more personal asceticism. Willingly doing what irks them, and it is just this we dwell on least, even in the Guides.'

It is good for young people, tempted to accept as authentic only those of life's crosses which they deliberately take on themselves, to be reminded of the Cross of Christ and of the significance of willing sacrifice. The tree is pruned that it may bear more fruit. There is no question of mutilation, but of full fruition—on the supernatural level.

There is, for the priest, a most important and happy task of education, in dealing with this trenchant criticism, and especially in pointing out another scale of values; as a young religious summed up the matter:

'Before entry, the spiritual Father has a very great part to play: he must not be afraid to reveal both the beauty and grandeur of the religious life, and all its difficulties.

Every girl must realise the depths of human wretchedness beforehand, if she is not subsequently to be frustrated in the common life.

She must know beforehand, in substance, to what her vows of Poverty, Chastity and Obedience will commit her.'

This thought brings us to our last point, the positive preparation of the candidate.

III   THE POSITIVE PREPARATION OF THE CANDIDATE

We must not be afraid to consider this from all possible angles.

A. THE PHYSICAL LEVEL

It is very important that the candidate should be fit, with reserves which she can draw on, if necessary, during the time of adjustment.

Avoid, therefore, any overdriving; recommend a rest before entering, forbid all mortifications and imprudent austerities.

Advise, to this end, a well-balanced and regular life (sleep, rest . . .).

'Certain professions', we are told, 'play havoc with our physical equilibrium, and one does not realise at the time what a handicap this can be. I think if one became a postulant in good physical condition, instead of living on one's nerves, it would be a great help.'

St Francis de Sales said: 'Do not emaciate Brother Ass before the time'.

B. The Practical Level

Do not neglect this aspect. It bears on the candidate's ability to be useful and to work for the common good of the community in the future. Just think how important the work of a community is, these days, to ensure its daily bread.

It is desirable, we are told, for girls to have at least the normal domestic accomplishments, to know how to embroider, sew and do dressmaking (not merely Church vestments): they are advised to have some gardening experience, to be able to cope intelligently with electricity, carpentry, and broken locks!

Need we mention the technical attainments, such as teaching, medicine, nursing and social work, which are brought into service, especially in the active congregations, and artistic attainments too, such as modelling, painting, drawing and singing, which can be so valuable in contemplative houses as well?

C. The Intellectual Level

Urge the candidate not to bury her talents, but gradually to complete her general education by reading, study circles and courses; to acquire a familiarity with Latin, so that she may have a better understanding of the Liturgy. Urge her to read for the type of diploma which might be useful to her in the congregation she is to enter.

'I am sorry', says a young sister, 'that I did not make use of the period of waiting before entry to pass my baccalauréat; a mistress of postulants whom I consulted on this matter only recommended some novels by Pierre l'Ermite.'

It would be a mistake to think that there will be more time and greater facilities later on. People in the world find it hard to appreciate how little time contemplatives have. But they must bear in mind that the day's timetable is broken up and severely curtailed by the Divine Office and other religious exercises. And, like families, convents are faced with all the usual chores of cooking and cleaning, not forgetting the care of the sick and the necessity of earning their daily bread.

Yet it is important to avoid dabbling in a subject, or playing on the surface. They must be advised to go deeply into it.

'The tendency today', we are told, 'is to read too much, without stopping to think and assimilate. One is then faced with the terrible contrast of a system directed towards meditation and silence, a silence which seems so terribly hard at the beginning of one's religious life!'

Another reply also notes the dilettantism, the intellectual dissipation characteristic of the age:

'We are so eager to know everything, to understand everything; and under the pretext of enrichment we read, or skim through, a multitude of books and reviews. We keep abreast of the latest films and plays, . . . we live in a hectic atmosphere, appearing to know everything because we have a smattering of everything, but in reality we have forgotten how to think, and are afraid of the mental effort involved in thinking for ourselves.'

D. THE PSYCHOLOGICAL LEVEL

Under this head comes the understanding of temperament and character, to assist the candidate's development. Urge young people to know themselves, their powers and limitations, so that they may subsequently be able to acquire balance, and be transformed. How many wounds, what friction and suffering could have been avoided or lessened in the common life, if the candidate had been made aware, in time, of its asperities, and of the chinks in its armour?

There is all the delicate and necessary work of schooling the emotions.

'My conception of the religious life', writes a young sister, 'and of married life, too, was very wide of the mark. This ignorance caused me to live my time as a postulant and a novice like a schoolgirl; I did not profit by these years as a woman would have done, since I was too anxious to gratify that desire to love and be loved, and to experience it. A deeper knowledge of life would have made it possible for me to approach the religious life as an ideal, straightaway, to look at it in the light of eternity, and not as a means of finding a higher and more certain happiness then the human happiness I was afraid of.'

The woman's vocation is a vocation of the heart. So she must know what loving, i.e. giving oneself, is, and encourage a growing sacrifice, the search for balance in and through the emotions, a joyful and willing temperance, learning in the school of our Lady to combine tenderness (Visitation, Cana) with strength (station at Calvary), those two great qualities of the heart.

Do not forget, in view of the whims and fancies which are so common in feminine society, to remind them of the discipline of the will (decision, energy, perseverance).

Finally, on the negative side, contemporary psychologists do ask that the least sign of any complex which might be liable to assume larger proportions in the convent (melancholy, defeatism, inferiority) should be disclosed, and an endeavour made to guard against it.

E. THE RELIGIOUS LEVEL

I said above that candidates should be concerned to lay foundations, rather than to anticipate their new way of life. Candidates must prepare themselves by an interior faithfulness to the divine call, by uprightness of life, and by an immediate acceptance of the will of God as revealed in the duties of their present state of life.

It is important that the priest himself should have a sound knowledge of, and high esteem for, the religious life if he is to impart it to aspirants. In fact, we are too ready these days to differentiate between religious life and the Christian life, whereas St Basil, the great legislator and master of Eastern monasticism, much preferred to compare them.

1. The religious life implies a real and strong Christian life already in being, i.e. a sense of God and the Christian mysteries:

'If I had understood then', writes a young nun, 'or if they had managed to make me understand that the religious life was above what I expected, that God was Wholly Other, I think it would have made the initial stages a good deal easier.'

The awareness of grace, of the dwelling of the Trinity in the soul:

'Why did someone not explain to me', says a young sister, 'exactly what is meant by *the soul's nuptials with Our Lord, contact with the person of Christ*, and why we are entitled really and truly to lay claim to it, and above all that it is not a matter of feeling? I was not at all prepared for this aspect of intimacy with our Lord, and this seems to me to be a fundamental point, which had its repercussions throughout my spiritual life.'

Understanding of the theological life:

'Learn', we are told, 'to live the present moment:

(i) *in faith,* for I can find the Lord this very day in events, in contacts with other people, in difficulties.

(ii) *in hope,* for it is the Lord himself who gives me strength to overcome these difficulties.

(iii) *in charity*, for it is by turning these little things or these great difficulties into opportunities for the love of God that the Lord gives me his very own love with which to love him.'

Prayer and the regular reception of the Sacraments:

'My director only ever asked two things of me', says a former Jociste: (*a*) to remember God frequently during the day, to attain to unceasing prayer. He called this "spiritual respiration". He wanted to make me see the uselessness of my efforts in so many directions if I did not introduce the love of God into them first of all, for it is the foundation of all spiritual progress. Despite all the various methods adopted, I remembered God very little.

(*b*) to go to Mass and to communicate every day, despite my little fervour, manifold distractions, and almost daily unpunctuality. I understand better now how important this costly effort was (Mass at 6.30 a.m., the Church a mile away). Was not this the best way of putting myself under the influence of God, of becoming stronger and more able to "will", and therefore to love, and to become personally involved, and also to see things more clearly?'

As to prayer, do not fail to point out that it is a life, and therefore made up of turning points, which the spiritual masters will help us to negotiate. As with any journey, the spiritual itinerary passes through varied country, sometimes fertile, sometimes barren (alternation of consolations and dryness, of God-consciousness and self-consciousness). Prudently initiate the candidate into meditation and mental prayer.

'I was staggered', says a sister, 'to find that postulants were permitted to meditate freely, and I did not know how to set about it profitably without letting my imagination stray into beautiful but fruitless thoughts. I do wish someone had instructed me beforehand.'

This schooling in prayer is, however, a delicate matter, for there are very many ways of approaching God, and both the movements of the Spirit in the individual soul, and the character of the congregation which the candidate will enter, must be respected.

It will be useful for the candidate to know of the various methods, so that she does not confer an 'absolute' character on the spirituality she has hitherto practised.

'It seems to me', says a young sister, 'that Guiding was a good remote preparation for me (it was the only movement I had any personal experience of); it gives some training in bodily discipline, poverty, service, generosity and love of one's neighbour. But we are not to think of the religious life as a mere continuation of Guide spirituality. The Guide promise cannot be compared with religious profession, which consecrates a creature to God.'

With regard to the sacraments, there is unquestionably room for some 'reappraisal' of the sacrament of penance, we are told.

'Personally', admits one sister, '—and I do not think my conduct was at all exceptional among my contemporaries—I used to communicate almost every day, but went for months without going to confession.'

Charity—the first and great commandment. But there is not only the active charity of good works, there is also the passive charity of tolerance, which is such a blessing in a community. Patience is a contemplative virtue of the highest degree, required by the *pati divina*, even before it is practised by one's companions.

Lastly, sense of the Church, its liturgical life and its apostolic responsibilities. It seems that modern youth is more alert to this, thanks particularly to Catholic Action.

We must emphasise the Christian life as the finest 'foundation' for the religious life, and the essential thing.

'The fact of envisaging the religious life as a deepening of the Christian life, which has already been lived in the world', writes a young professed nun, 'would have lessened the impression of a leap into the unknown; I should have seen this transition not so much as a break, an abandonment of the joys, beauties and values of secular life (family, friends, professional, social, cultural and artistic activities), as a re-shaping of these values to bend and live them all to God.'

2. It remains true, however, that the religious life is its own way a new life; even if profession is regarded as a complement of baptism, a reinforcement of its claims, a new Pasch, it is also a special way of holiness through the evangelical counsels. It implies a special call and its own special response. There will have to be a break with the old and faith in the new—and this is true of any vocation, as is classically illustrated in the pages of Scripture by the call of Abraham.

But one must be careful not to separate the vows from charity, of which they are, in a sense, the wings.

While it is true that the religious life is determined by the letter of the vows, it is no less a preferential love, a response to the Gospel's 'if thou wilt', a love which both animates the letter and finds expression in it.

The vows have already been mentioned earlier, so I shall raise only one point here. What are we to say about a private vow of chastity before entry into religion? The director should be sure about the candidate's innermost motives, for there are two possible psychological reasons—love of God, or fear of life.

3. Modern youth and the religious life.

Is there anything to be gained, in concluding, by considering again the mind of modern youth, whose apprehensions about the religious life have already been mentioned, and underlining the points which the priest would do well to emphasise, to make the transition from the world to the religious life a little easier?

No purpose is served by comparing generations, for all have their qualities and their defects. No purpose is served by stressing the traps into which they may fall—formerly it was pharisaism, today it is cynicism. It is better to try to help mutual understanding in a supernatural charity, which transcends antagonisms by putting things in the context which explains them. Young people today have a spontaneous charm and simplicity and loyalty which must come from a genuine love of truth. It is in the name of this truth that we shall perhaps manage to convince them most easily of their need for humility and faith.

(i) *Humility*

On this point a young sister writes:

'Let young people not be so sure that they understand themselves, that they understand everything; let them come more humbly, more submissively, into the religious life; let them make an effort to understand others, and to appreciate their worth.'

It could not have been better said.

Young people are too conceited about their generation, too possessed by their own outlook, as if it gave a faultless explanation of the absolute; in short, they have an assurance, a confidence in themselves which would border on pride if they were aware of it. It is a sign of the times, and the mark of men intoxicated by their discoveries and their advancing ascendancy over the forces of nature; so much so that they forget the Creator who has entrusted this lordship to them.

It is very necessary for them to rediscover, in religion if they have not done so previously, the gospel precept that we are all unprofitable servants. The disciple is not above his Master, and the *exaltavit* of Christ implies the *exinanivit*. But it is perhaps not so much the independence of the young as their lack of humility and faith which is the obstacle to their obedience. An intellectual pride which wants to understand everything, and everything to be explained; the will re-echoes this by refusing any yoke which it might not have recognised, and which might impose restraints and limits on development. Let the priest endeavour to convince pre-postulants that on entering religion they have first of all to receive. They readily see what they

themselves are bringing, and indeed they are ready to offer it generously. They are surprised that they are not thanked more for the gift
of themselves which they are making to the congregation. They are
even scandalised when superiors make a show of hesitation. They
forget that entry into religion is not the result of a unilateral decision—
their own—and that compared with the Order's spiritual teaching,
traditions and patrimony of sanctity, their own little personality
scarcely counts.

They have better things to do than sit in judgment; for indeed, by
their criticisms, they risk sinking the ship which has accepted them.

Let them be loyal, acquiescing with simplicity in the loss of the
defects of their qualities, which will only shine with greater radiance
on a community which they will thus have won over.

(ii) Faith

They will not attain humility without a faith pinned on the rock of
Christ and his Church. In an age eager for efficiency, for immediate
and tangible success, it is certainly difficult to consent to share in the
apparent failure of the Cross, to rally to the paradox of the Beatitudes.
But we must die to live, and lose to gain.

'On entering', writes a young sister, 'I knew that the crux of the problem
was to be found in the renunciation of self, to leave the way open for God.
What I did not know was that dying to self is such a long and difficult process
. . . there is a brutal change effected in our life. We awake to find ourselves
in complete dependence, without responsibility and without initiative (bear in
mind, nevertheless, that the reversal could not be borne without some spark
of heroism!). The leap into the gaping void is indispensable (faith!); you have
got to have unshakeable confidence, tremendous love in your heart, and—wait
and see. Later, after the years of formation, balance will be restored; a new
balance in which all things will be rediscovered, in a different fashion and
purified!'

The ideal has still to be embodied in the triviality of little everyday
actions, in the monotony of humble duties, and the drabness of the
daily round. It is in this context, so disconcerting and lacking in glory,
that the reshaping of the new man is effected. The young should realise
this before entering, so that they may be able to rekindle the lamp of
their faith from the Lamb who will be their Light, and that they may
'know how to do little things', as Pascal says, 'as if they were great,
because of the majesty of Jesus Christ who is performing them through
us'; and indeed, should they become superiors one day, to 'know how
to do great things as if they were but small things, because of his
almighty power'.

We all feel small and inadequate, faced with the high and delicate task of the education of those whom the Lord has chosen for himself. It needs patience, kindness and moderation, progressively measuring out, as Christ himself did with the Apostles, both teaching and burden. *You cannot bear them now!* Again, like Christ, we can count on the Spirit to perfect the work that we have begun:

> Come o father of the poor
> Ever bounteous of thy store
> Come our hearts' unfailing light.

FR JULIEN-PAUL DE LA VIÈRGE, O.D.C.

PART TWO

PRACTICE

CHAPTER VI

THE PRIEST'S ROLE IN THE CONFESSIONAL

I HAVE been asked to speak to you about the awakening of religious vocation through the confessional because several girls to whom I have given spiritual advice are known to have become religious. I am the curate of a parish in Paris, in which my particular responsibility is work amongst the boys, but for several years I have had charge of a number of girls' organisations.

I have not questioned other priests about the subject with which we are concerned. I shall, therefore, give you a personal rather than a technical report, which will reflect a simple priest's faith in the value of the confessional as a means of helping souls to hear God's call.

I have prepared my subject particularly with girls of sixteen or over in mind. I have made use of Fr Chevignard's paper, both in method and expression. He told us that the divine call is a mystery. I have tried to look at the subject from this point of view. And as I am only going to speak about the priest's part in awakening vocations, I shall stop when the penitent asks the question: 'Have I a vocation?'.

Very often the circumstances which have made it possible for a soul to hear the call of God are many and varied, and the priest has his place in most of them. Others will speak to you about the priest's role in various situations, at school, in the parish, in organisations and retreats. For that reason I have tried to narrow the subject as far as possible so as to speak only about the specific contact which we have with the penitent in the confessional. It seems to me, in fact, that in the confessional a soul finds itself, or ought to find itself, in a more trusting and humble frame of mind than anywhere else, and that consequently it is more ready there than elsewhere to hear the Lord's call. Therefore we ought to make our function as instruments of the Lord, as effective as possible in the confessional.

We must know:

1. How to prepare ourselves to be good instruments of the divine call.

2. How to cultivate the religious attitude in our penitents, which will enable them to hear the divine call.

I How to Prepare Ourselves for our Role in the Confessional

A. REMOTE PREPARATION

First of all, our remote preparation. This will include:

1. A very regular revision of our theology. Very often, after a few years, our theological knowledge becomes extremely stereotyped. So it is good for us, instead of simply taking up our seminary notes again, to read a new theological book, or even to borrow a young priest's notes. This will compel us to re-think our theology in the light of new ideas which are more adapted to the thought of the Church at the present time, and to the trends of thought in the modern world.

2. A knowledge which is ever mindful of the great currents of spirituality, and at the same time a knowledge of the new Orders, such as the Little Sisters of Fr de Foucauld and the Berengères.

If we are to be instruments of the Lord, we must not be tied to one tradition of spirituality. Of course each of us has his own spirituality; one aspect of Christ will attract us more than others; but the will of the Lord for a particular penitent will not necessarily coincide with the will of the Lord for ourselves, and all too easily we are in danger of being not the instruments of Christ, but selfish technicians.

3. A profound understanding of the spiritual foundations of the principal Christian movements. So, when a penitent informs us that she is a Guide, a Jociste, a Child of Mary, we shall not be in danger of criticising the movement to which she belongs, but shall be in a position to help her to put the accent on those spiritual values which she will find in it.

4. A knowledge of the inner meaning of the great values of the religious life, such as obedience, poverty, chastity, the common life, public prayer, the missionary spirit. This understanding we shall only acquire through meditation and prayer. We shall then be in a position to justify their necessity to our penitents, not by philosophical reasoning nor by purely human ascesis, but by completely theological argument. This is all the more necessary because in the confessional one has to be accurate, simple and speedy.

B. Immediate Preparation

Remote preparation is incomplete without more immediate preparation. We must place ourselves in the presence of God before hearing confessions. Lengthy prayer is not necessary, but it is essential to remind ourselves that we are going to perform a liturgical act, and to speak in the name of God.

Similarly, while we are hearing confessions we ought to place ourselves in the presence of God again. You know the danger of losing one's calm, either because one is overwhelmed by a flow of words or because of the very painful nature of the recital or the nervous strain. Now, patience ought to be one of the confessor's virtues, and he will only obtain it by asking it of God, and by remembering that he is the instrument of God. To lose patience and cut off a penitent in the middle of his confession very often makes it quite impossible for him to go on.

Without this preparation and this repeated placing of ourselves in the presence of God, we are in danger of becoming machines for dispensing absolutions, or informed psychologists, and not spiritual *fathers*. If we are not imbued with this spiritual paternity we are hardly in a position to help a soul to discern the call of God, because our penitents will be only too aware of the human element in us.

I have met a follower of Georges Roux, the so-called 'Christ of Montfavet', on several occasions, and on one of them I had a long and extremely frank conversation with her. I asked her why she had left the Catholic religion. She made an evasive reply. Two days later I had a long letter from her. Here are some extracts from it:

'I was a little embarrassed, but my hesitation about replying verbally was simply due to some scruple which paralysed me and kept back everything which should have come pouring out spontaneously. I was afraid of hurting your feelings by appearing to "attack" the Church. One can so often do so much harm without wanting to, by a single clumsy word . . .

However, I want you to know that it is by no means my intention to criticise, still less to judge, the religion in which I was brought up, and which I loved very deeply. . . . It was no longer the voice of God I heard behind the grille of the confessional, but the voice of a minister practising a "trade", with little concern for the simple soul who expected him to be the representative of God.'

II   How to Help our Penitents to Accept The Call

I have tried to show you how we can prepare ourselves to be of assistance to our penitents in the confessional. I am now going to deal with helping our young penitents to hear God's call.

Briefly, it seems to me to be necessary to make them aware first of all of the fundamental call of baptism, as Fr Chevignard said. So I shall divide this second part into three headings:

A. Who is calling? or Knowing God.

B. To what does he call?—I shall stress the ministerial aspect—or Knowing Others.

C. Whom does he call? or Knowing Oneself.

First of all, I ought to tell you that in preparation for this conference I re-read the report given three years ago by Abbé Baechler of the diocese of Nancy, on ordinary and extra-ordinary confessors. Many of his remarks can also be applied to penitents who have already begun to experience some stirring of religious vocation. I shall quote only one:

'In hearing the case submitted to his judgment, the confessor may have occasion to question. And he will be right. In my opinion, the dialogue form is excellent, for it breaks the ritual monotony and formalism of too many confessions. But he must be careful not to go outside the limits imposed by his function . . .'[1]

So, starting with the penitent's own words, we can try to arouse that spiritual awareness we would like to see in each one of them. If the penitent refuses the dialogue method, we must not insist on it, for this might offend; nor is there any magic formula for us: we must remain fatherly, and try to adapt ourselves to that particular soul.

Now let us examine in greater detail the way in which this awakening to God's fundamental call in baptism is to be effected.

A. WHO IS CALLING?

We can sometimes perceive from the penitent's own words that she has not even realised who God is. Her confession, for example, takes the form of a list of offences corresponding to the commandments of God or to the examination of conscience in her catechism. There is no connection at all between her sins, and they are all on the same level. She feels guilty because she has broken the law. For her, God is a rule rather than a Person. Such a confession is not false in itself, but it is very imperfect. We must try to focus the confession on the main point, which is lack of love for God. No one really loves a legalistic God; we could not give our lives to him.

In attempting to discover why a particular penitent has a wrong attitude to God, we usually find that there are various reasons for it:

[1] *The Direction of Nuns*, p. 142, Aquin Press.

(i) The penitent has a wrong idea of God because her religious instruction came to an end when she was twelve or thirteen. Her development is unbalanced; her instruction in other subjects has gone on, particularly if she is a student, but her instruction in religious matters has not proceeded accordingly. We ought therefore to lay upon her the serious obligation of taking up her religious instruction again. She must be advised either to read, or to join some group where she would receive appropriate religious teaching. You know as well as I do that such a person is in danger of having doubts against faith sooner or later, if she has not already had them.

(ii) Occasionally a Christian girl will deliberately maintain what she describes as peasant faith partly because it is such a fine thing: but it is also much easier. Here again we ought to point out to her that her ties with God can scarcely be called filial. When we love our father, we are eager to know him; when our father has given us a present, we only use it to give pleasure to others. God has given us a mind so that we may know him better. People are often quite content to take advantage of the definition of mystery—'A truth revealed by God, which we are to believe, though we cannot understand it'—so that they can resignedly shelter behind this impossibility. We must stress, then, the love of the Father who reveals himself to us.

(ii) But, this knowledge of the God who reveals himself is a trifling thing if it exists only in the intellect; that is why I should be inclined to look for a further indication of the knowledge of God in the way a person prays (*lex orandi, lex credendi*). Does your penitent pray? How does she pray? The answer to these questions will be easily found in the confession itself. She has not always said 'her' prayers. She feels guilty about not having prayed, in the same way as she would if caught poking a blazing fire. First of all, we shall try to make her realise that she is guilty, not because she has not said 'her' prayers, but because she has not prayed, because she has not talked to God her Father. Just as it is not enough to say 'Good-morning' and 'Good-night' to your father and mother without thinking what you are saying, and without saying a word to them the rest of the time if you live with them, so, to behave as children towards God, it is not enough always to recite the same prayers mechanically. We shall try to lead such a penitent to a more personal and meditative prayer. We shall speak to her about interior silence, converse with God, and praying the psalms.

Other indications of a defective religious knowledge of God are the way in which the penitent accuses herself of having missed Mass, or of allowing distractions during Mass . . . a rather magical way of thinking of prayer and the sacraments.

B. TO WHAT DOES HE CALL?

This religious knowledge of God will give us a sense of belonging to him. God has not created us merely for himself, but for others as well, and so we will now see what our penitent is called upon to do.

How can she be given a true understanding of others, and an apostolic and ministerial way of looking at things?

Here again, our penitent's own words will guide us. A confession concentrating exclusively on duties towards God and the capital sins may prompt us to ask: 'And what about your neighbour? Is everything in order there?' Young people will rarely reply: 'Oh yes, father, I do not concern myself with other people at all, so everything must be all right—I never do them any harm'. They will not say so, but it is often easy enough to see that their relationship with others is restricted to not doing them any harm. They feel no responsibility at all towards other people, so we must help them to discover God's plan for creation, and the part which each one of us has to play in it. The actual sins confessed will give us the clue; for example: 'I have omitted my prayers'. We shall go on then to speak of prayer one for another, of the Mystical Body of Christ and the responsibility of the baptised to pray daily for and in the place of those who do not pray.

Or again: 'I have been lazy at work'. God gives us everything we have; God gives us time—but for the special work among others which he has in mind for us.

Generally speaking, we should advise a penitent who has made an egocentric confession to interest himself in other people, to mix with them, to know them. Occasionally our penitents will say: 'But I am interested in others. . . . I am a Guide captain, I visit old people'. But the confession reveals that her love for others is extremely selective. Apart from those who have been singled out, no one is known or loved at all. We must help her to understand that 'knowing others' does not depend on her own inclinations, but it is determined by God himself. Wherever a person lives, she must be a centre of charity. To help a penitent who cannot see beyond herself to discover other people, it is sometimes necessary to send her to visit the really wretched.

She must be urged to join some apostolic Catholic group. To know people with an understanding love, it is not enough merely to 'see' them. Certain penitents will really try to 'see' the people around them, but they will not come to love them. Some will say so quite plainly; but others will think they love them, and will no longer accuse themselves of any failure towards others. To the first, we shall counsel patience, abnegation and humility. We shall ask them to unite themselves more closely to Christ, so that they may be imbued with his love and his spirit of sacrifice.

With the second group we shall be patient, awaiting the opportunity for pointing out to them their want of true love for others. It will be some particular sin of anger or malice, or perhaps of jealousy or impurity, which will enable us to point out that, without being aware of it, our penitent has not really loved all her fellow-creatures, that there were those towards whom she harboured some wilful resentment, or for whom she thought she could do nothing, either because they found it impossible to change or because they were too wicked for anyone to condescend to be interested in them. Here again, we shall begin by making them pray for others, and learn that they are not to judge but to help.

C. Whom Does God Call?

We have seen how we can help our penitents to know God and their fellow-creatures in God, but so far the impression may have been given that God calls all our penitents in the same way. So in order to make it quite clear that God has a particular call for each one, we must now ask: 'Whom does God call?' Fr Chevignard reminded us that God's call was a personal thing, and that it was present from birth. This call takes into account individual temperament, defects and qualities; and if it is to be discerned the penitent must have a thorough knowledge of herself.

For this she must regularly examine her conscience, and regularly make use of the sacrament of penance. We should, then, help our penitents first of all to make their own personal rule about frequency of confession. Then, with them, we shall look for the fundamental source of their faults, either their major defect or the actual tendency in them which brings it about. Very often, for example, we shall find that anger springs from pride; gluttony and laziness from a certain cowardice, lack of courage or general carelessness. All this will make us want to help the penitent to acquire some will-power.

Our penitents, like ourselves, are often not unified personalities; and we have to help them to discover this lack of unity in themselves, and to try to understand why they are so unstable and divided. To this end we shall begin with the subject matter of their own confessions, to show them that their minds are in certain circumstances dominated by their bodies, that their opinions are not really their own and free, but are dominated by their environment and therefore by the world. Often this lack of unity means that, either consciously or unconsciously, they want to have the joys both of this world and of God.

It is not enough merely to urge young people to know themselves and to dispel their illusions about themselves by pointing out the fundamental causes of their faults; we must also make them aware of their qualities and the gifts which God has given them. Some confessions make us exclaim: 'What graces you have received!' We must then go on to show that it is not enough merely to avoid evil, but that we must do good, and will it. For example, we could say, à propos of poverty, 'Check all expenses; know how to use your money'; or, à propos of obedience, 'Be careful to be exact and disciplined, even in little things, to ask advice about reading, etc.'

Other confessions will reveal an appreciation of the beautiful, some artistic talent, and we must direct this towards the attainment of a sense of real beauty, towards the perfecting of created nature in the penitent herself; and it is easy to relate this to purity and chastity.

We may also find penitents with great generosity, an easy ability to share the unhappiness of others; and we must develop this by asking more of them than of others, pointing out to them that what may be a very light fault in others could in their own case be sheer egoism and a very serious want of love for others.

I have spoken about 'who is calling' and 'what he is calling our penitents to do'. We must now try to help the penitent to answer the question 'Who am I?' If she has come all this way without faltering, she will now have to face the crucial question: 'Is God calling me?'

Some souls will have travelled almost all the way alone. When we first come into contact we ask: 'Have you considered devoting your whole life to God?', and very often the answer is, 'Yes, but I am not sure'. Others will struggle slowly along gradually accepting the fact that they must give their whole life to God, often asking, 'Why me?'

Since it is a very serious thing to ask: 'Have you thought about your vocation?' in the confessional, we must be prudent about it, but with a supernatural prudence which is not cowardice. If the penitent jibs, we have to explain gently without labouring the point that what we mean is consecration to God. Sometimes, when we see that our penitent is a very generous soul, that she really wishes to do everything for God, and that she appears to have no intention of getting married, we can then—obviously with much caution—put to her the possibility of taking private vows, e.g. for a year. I have known several penitents who themselves asked to be allowed to take private vows, and who had no idea at all at that time of becoming religious. But they are now.

There is undoubtedly much more to be said on this subject. I have only dealt with what I try to do myself. It is obviously much easier to say what should be done than to do it. But I believe we must all treat more seriously the encounter souls have with God, through our ministry, and we must always believe that the Lord is calling many souls to consecrate themselves wholly to him.

ABBÉ LUCIEN LAUDE,
Curate of Saint-Jacques du Haut-Pas, Paris.

CHAPTER VII

THE ROLE OF THE PRIEST IN AWAKENING VOCATIONS AT SCHOOL

THE EXPERIENCE of twelve years' ministry which has, in part, been devoted to preaching retreats in educational establishments for girls, does not entitle me to call myself an expert. I am therefore compelled to limit the subject which I have been given to the type of school about which I know most, the independent secondary schools.

Some very fine vocations have come from State secondary schools. Retreats made by their best pupils, either at school or at some Abbey or Retreat House, have been a powerful factor in these vocations, even where they have not been directly responsible for them. Holiday Camps have proved fertile ground, too. Four hundred girls representing the schools of France and North Africa spent a month together at the Pralognan Camp in 1956, which was a fine demonstration of Christian strength.

Independent primary and technical schools have produced some magnificent vocations, too. Many appear to me to owe the persistence and progress of their fervour to the family, of course, but devotional organisations such as the French Children of Mary (whose impressive annual reunion on 11th November is attended, I am told, by ten to twelve thousand girls), the Guide movement and those forms of Catholic Action which are compatible with the life of primary and technical schools have helped cure self-centredness and given the girls an awareness of others.

Here and there Christian movements have penetrated the State primary and technical schools; French law, which does not permit chaplains as such to be appointed to these schools, is partly responsible for the religious ignorance pervalent here, and consequently, apart from the special intervention of God, for the very limited number of women's vocations from these schools. You will be aware of the efforts of Abbés Dutil and Girand to adapt and present the Gospel in terms suitable to such circles. *Votre Messe, Votre Vie* was the first attempt at this, and it has been followed by several others.

As I have not had time to look into the statistics for this type of school, I am compelled to restrict my observations to the independent secondary schools; but here again, I have to limit my subject.

In these schools many different means are employed to promote the fostering of vocations, but I am not concerned to describe them. I shall confine myself to how the priest can discern the vocations thus awakened. There appear to be two special occasions particularly involved:

(1) The annual three-day retreat at the beginning of the academic year (this may take place any time between October and February), and (2) (a novelty which merits discussion), the school-leaving retreat for girls; the Dominicans at Mortefontaine, by inviting the students of philosophy from their numerous French houses, seem to have given this retreat its most accomplished form.

Eight questions present themselves:

I Is it opportune, in a retreat, to devote an entire sermon to religious vocation?

II How can we recognise the vocation?

III How can we follow up a potential vocation?

IV What are the principal conditions for the development of a vocation which has already been decided upon?

V Are there any books to help the priest to become a good diagnoser of women's vocations?

VI Are statistics able to indicate the influence of devotional and direct evangelical action movements on the growth of vocations?

VII In what way has Catholic Action influenced the esteem in which religious vocations are held?

VIII Are teaching sisters in charge of schools where vocations occur justified in their fears that the flow of vocations for the congregation which has been responsible for the education of these girls will dry up?

I Is it Opportune to Devote an Entire Sermon to Religious Vocation in a Retreat?

Opinion is divided. There are those who think that sermons on our duty to God, on fidelity to the spirit of the Gospel and the need for sacrifice will be quite sufficient to cover the subject. 'Love God, and do what you will.' They ask why we should raise a problem which will often be no more than external—habit or no habit?—and suggest it is better to insist on the needs of men's souls, thus stimulating a universal zeal, directed through prayer and action. To speak to girls about religious vocation is a subtle way of turning their thoughts inwards on themselves, instead of making them aware of others. 'As a result of the retreat you preached to us at X', a young girl wrote to me, 'my egoism increased: there was God and myself—and the rest.'

Moreover, some maintain that the devotion to our Lord which is thus promoted is infected with sentimentality. They say that to direct girls into Catholic Action, to concrete charity in all its forms, is much better than to compel a student of philosophy or rhetoric to ask herself, 'Shall I be a religious? And where?'

But the reception accorded by the girls themselves to sermons on vocation, in many different kinds of retreat, does not seem to me to support this view.

It is my belief that the Christian girl who has no ties cannot avoid asking herself several questions when she thinks about her future; first as to her state: 'Where can I practise more purely, more surely, more permanently, the greatest possible charity towards God and my neighbour?'

If she feels in her soul a special love for the Person of Jesus, she will ask a second question: 'What does "following Jesus" mean?' To which the answer is: 'It means committing oneself to his service without any guarantee other than his word, and without any conditions other than the certainty of receiving a special grace to perfect the holocaust' (cf Fr de Montcheuil, *Problèmes de Vie Spirituelle*, vol. 1: *L'obligation d'etre parfait*, Chap. V). Fr de Montcheuil notes that one of the vices of modern youth, influenced by Gide, is the refusal to commit oneself. Young people want to place themselves at the disposal of God, but also want to remain as it were free lances, not bound by vows to some definite institution. So if the soul wishes to know or develop the most perfect love of Jesus, the priest will be compelled to point out that a vow of chastity is required, and that if she wishes to be an offering herself, then obedience to Jesus will be the submission of her whole life to him in a way of life canonically approved by the Church. Any possibility of going back would be a kind of reservation in a gift which love instinctively knows should be total.

When the preacher has dealt quite simply with fundamental themes,

'Why were you created?' or 'How far would you go to show Jesus how utterly faithful your love for him is?', he will find that he is obliged to broach the question of religious vocation.

A third point is noted by Edith Stein in her book *Frauenbildung und Frauenberufe*:

'And because we have to see the normal development in the vocation of physical motherhood, we should adapt the normal type of feminine education to this end. Nevertheless, since even those whose natural aptitude points to this are not at all certain that they will be able to achieve it, they should also be trained for the other way. Natural aptitude for celibacy is exceptional. Yet the vocation to be virgins consecrated to God is not given only to those with a natural disposition for it. Today many are called to remain unmarried whose nature and inclinations had seemed to destine them for the other way. Education must provide for all these cases, so that the call of God, which may be made as clear by external circumstances as by the inclination of the heart, should be accepted neither rebelliously nor resignedly, but with willing co-operation.'[1]

Since it may assume the form of a strong and joyful acceptance of a state which is none the less opposed to natural inclinations, the call of God ought to be explained and proclaimed in every possible way. The spirituality of the 'handmaid of the Lord' ought in any event to occupy the central place in the retreat, and, with all due respect for the sanctity of marriage, girls should hear in one form or another a commentary on Chapter VII of the first epistle to the Corinthians, which expresses what the Council of Trent later confirmed (Denzinger 981): the essential superiority of virginity over the married state. In his discourse to the Superiors General on 2nd August 1953, Pius XII stressed the responsibility before God and the Church of those who for some years, despite the warnings of the Church and contrary to her mind, have conceded to marriage a fundamental superiority over virginity; who go so far even as to present it as the only means of ensuring the development and natural fulfilment of human personality.

The girl who makes a retreat ought to feel that we priests are conscious of our responsibility in this matter.

With this in mind, when and how should the question of vocation be presented in a three-day retreat? How are we to set about giving it?

When I know my audience well, these are the headings of my instructions for the first day:

First Instruction: God. His love for us. Our response to this love.

Writings of Edith Stein, edited and translated by Hilda Graef, Peter Owen, London, 1956, p. 158.

Second Instruction: Salvation—adopting the best means to holiness.

Third Instruction: First way of holiness—Marriage.

Fourth Instruction: The royal path of sacrifice—Consecrated Virginity.

The practical advantage of this method is that it enables the girl to ask herself the question sufficiently early in the retreat for her to seek advice during the retreat itself.

When I am less sure of my audience, after the sermons on the meaning of life I broach the problem raised by sin (which amounts to saying 'No' to God) and by hell; then I deal with marriage and motherhood (the normal way of sanctity for women): 'She shall be saved through child-bearing' (1 Tim. 2, 15), however one may interpret the text. Only then do I tackle Chapter 10 of St Mark's Gospel, and present the call of the rich man and the urgent words of Christ: 'One thing is wanting unto thee'.

In addition, the conference on vocation to the religious life, coming after the general confession of sins, then finds its logical place: 'I can make reparation for my past life in this form of total self-offering'. This desire to make reparation is not without its dangers in the case of people with vivid imagination. But it is an excellent stimulant to real generosity: 'Sanctity', says Fr Faber, 'springs from love, but from a love which is itself born of pardon'.

The conference, then, in this second scheme, will be given on the second evening of a three-day retreat.

Having raised the subject, how are we to make the girls see that it may be *their splendid destiny as women* to become religious? (This is the title of a book by Paula Hoesl on the missionary vocation of women.)

At this point it is necessary to consider what St Ignatius describes thus:

'three times, in each of which a sound and good election may be made.

The first time is when God our Lord so moves and attracts the will, that, without doubt or the power of doubting, such a devoted soul follows what has been pointed out to it, as St Paul and St Matthew did when they followed Christ our Lord.

The second time is when much light and knowledge is obtained by experiencing consolations and desolations, and by experience of the discernment of various spirits.

The third time is one of tranquillity: when one considers, first, for what man is born, viz., to praise God our Lord, and to save his soul; and when, desiring this, he chooses as the means to this end a kind of life within the bounds of the Church, in order that he may thereby be helped to serve God our Lord and to save his soul. I said a time of tranquillity; that is, when the soul is not agitated by divers spirits, but enjoys the use of its natural powers freely and quietly.'[1]

Occasionally God intimates the character of his message by some quasi miraculous shock. I remember, when I was sixteen experiencing a great shock at the first Congress for recruitment to the priesthood, when I heard Colonel Rollin, a Commander of the *Légion d'Honneur* and father of ten children, tell the story of his vocation to the priesthood. He was applauded by the two thousand five hundred members of the Congress present at Stanislas. Spiritual shocks such as this have their proper place in helping to form a generous resolution.

Or, God may quietly press the cause of total generosity through those spiritual sorrows and joys which are experienced when this question of one's future arises, both in the course of daily life and during the retreat itself. (Feelings of joy and sorrow are of course to be interpreted with great discretion.)

Or he may impart to the soul such judgment as will enlighten the mind at the right moment. Thus, a student of the Polytechnic who has a brilliant mind but little piety may, by the needs of some missionary country, quietly find himself asking: 'Why should this not be me?'

The danger is that girls tend to dismiss this approach by saying: 'Oh, no miracle has brought me a vocation. Our Lord has not thrown me from my horse like St Paul, or taken me by the hair like Habacuc. . . . Vocation simply does not appeal to me.' And so they wrongly infer that they have not been called to the religious life. The supernatural call to care for lepers can be a very different thing from a natural bent. 'If I have any vocation at all', they conclude, 'it is some reasonable vocation such as a prudent marriage. Better not to think about it at all.'

The real difficulty for those concerned, as well as for the director himself, is to see the connection between the sanctity—and often simply the salvation—of the soul, and entry into religion. So, may I refer to those words of St Bernard, in which he says that the religious life exists for two kinds of people: weak souls who are unable to live in a state of grace in the world, and strong souls whose craving for the infinite cannot be satisfied by the world.

I should explain that by weak souls are not meant those incorrigible cases which are rejected before solemn vows, but those in whom God has instilled a healthy dread of the world as a vehicle of sin; those who

[1] *The Spiritual Exercises of St Ignatius*, Burns Oates & Washbourne, 1908, p. 56.

have learnt by personal experience of their own tendencies and failings.

This radical knowledge of their own weakness is, in the words of mystical theologians such as Schram, impossible 'without a strictly transcendent illumination' (*Theologia Mystica*, 1).

It goes without saying that any response to a grace appealing to the entire will for a decision which will commit the subject to complete self-sacrifice, must rest on strictly transcendent motives.

These appear to me to be the principal points in reply to the first question: should we give a whole sermon on vocation in order to make the girls think about it?

II   How Can we Recognise the Call?

The general principles underlying any answer to this question were discussed at this Conference three years ago.[1]

I shall only add one point: even if the girls have furnished me with guarantees as to their health, their generosity and their good sense; even if I have been completely satisfied by the answers in reply to the seven or eight questionnaires which, in the free time between instructions, the retreatants, sometimes with considerable embarrassment, agree to supply; even after all these assurances, I consider it indispensable to know whether they love and practise private prayer, and are regular and frequent in their attendance at Mass and Holy Communion.

The quasi-certainty that a girl will be capable of accepting and following a vocation is only given me when I have evidence that this fervour is either already a positive fact or, at any rate, seriously promised.

True enough, there are conversions, even—I was going to say, particularly—during retreats made in the undergraduate period. And of those converted, some may contemplate the religious life.

A taste for adventure or even a craving for greatness (*Caritas magna operetur*) may, alas, be deceptive. What has frequently limited my confidence has been the poverty of the moral soil on which the vocation has to grow. I can sense that prayer and the eucharistic spirit are not firmly rooted in the heart. On the contrary, their conversation betrays scepticism, cheap tastes, timid and common-place little minds,

[1] *Doctrinal Instruction of Nuns*, Aquin Press, 1956.

a nervous system scarcely capable of bridling the urge for the cinema, dances or guilty pleasures or of preventing the return of old disorders, those internal enemies which manifestly poison any vocation, even though this is often frankly desired and the girl has actually mentioned it in confidence to her friends.

We feel rather uneasy about some of these confidences: this girl may not be deceiving me today, but will she do so tomorrow?

Even in those cases where I have been in doubt about the spiritual or moral qualities of the retreatant, I have found it difficult to say to her: 'I cannot really believe in your vocation'. But it seemed too easy to say: 'Another spiritual father will judge your case in another retreat'. I usually stick to the reply: 'Keep to a strict rule of Communion. Tell me in six months' time if you have communicated earnestly, and what has happened about the call you have heard.' It is not right either to give too much encouragement, or yet to abandon those who have thus put themselves in our hands.

For those girls, on the other hand, who seem to fulfil every condition, it is necessary to ensure that the retreat is followed up. This brings us to the question of dealing with the perseverance of those vocations which have been decided on at school, and in which factors external to the vocation itself crop up to delay entry into a congregation.

III   HOW ARE WE TO FOLLOW UP A VOCATION?

1. If the retreat preacher is certain that he is able to do it himself, then let him try, by means of wise direction, to assist grace. But as a rule this is not possible. That is why, in my opinion, we can advance no resolution more important than this: 'Promise to make a strict retreat for three, five or six days every year (this is a first-rate piece of advice, very simple, but very often omitted). Write down this resolution, but be sure that you consider beforehand what your own personal, family and professional commitments are likely to be.'

2. Make sure that the girl's friendly connection with the congregation of her choice is maintained. On the pretext of not wanting to fetter her liberty, some institutes have not kept up their contact with the candidate during her adolescence. A maternal Church should 'send a breath of fresh air to counteract the stifling atmosphere of those anaemic 3 a.m. surprise parties!' It is the work of Catholic Action

to deal with this. But religious, be they contemplatives, teachers, nurses or missionaries, will all have their own way of helping in this work.

Each congregation has its own characteristic expression, and every religious, through her joy, will be a danger to the Prince of this world: 'Terribly dangerous', affirmed Mgr Sloskan, then in Siberia, 'are the files of the O.G.P.U., in that there he is presented with the spectacle of joy in suffering.'

Any religious who loves and shows her attachment to the Institute ensures that moral certainty in the heart of the candidate that she too will attain balance in the religious life. A novice held on through a very difficult time because a thirty-year-old religious, foreseeing her future struggles, had told her in confidence: 'During my novitiate I wept every night'. Which signified: 'It is very hard. But after the bitter rind, the fruit will be very sweet to taste.' This religious, now of considerable influence, proves by her joy that she triumphed over her phase of tears.

To encourage introductions to abbeys and novitiates, to give sound explanations about the spirituality of the various congregations, seems to be one of the first duties of the teacher of souls—this applies to every priest, but specially to boarding school chaplains. Although they are often old, they can, if they are blessed with intuition and the necessary literature, almost without any effort beyond presenting the required information, safely direct the vocations of girls, who, if I may say so, will gradually choose for themselves from what they have learnt.

Cardinal Mercier arranged a whole course of instruction by pictures illustrating the steps to the priesthood and the various parts of the Mass. We owe it to the Church to have films about the congregations, talks by missionaries, and volumes of biography available. Who has need of religious to continue the work? *Ignoti nulla cupido*. Canon Blanadet, in publishing letters from religious describing the origin and development of their vocations, in his book *Risquer la vie pour Dieu* has filled a need.

Fr Delbrel in 1907 pleaded for the inclusion in the catechism of a chapter specifically devoted to the evangelical counsels and the religious state. Our present catechisms do not quite meet this wish; 'missionary' is not a word our catechisms use.

3. Interest families in the gift of their child. St Ambrose praised both

the gift of a consecrated virgin and what her mother does for God each day with this gift.[1] The period between the decision and its fulfilment is always a dangerous one, and the priest who has been asked to contact the family at such a time must be armed. One of our classical trials (we must try to eradicate it) is the injunction of one or other of the parents to the girl: 'Your retreat preacher has filled your head with this idea of vocation; I forbid you to speak or write to him.' And this edict may rest on considerations which are sometimes not very flattering to the priest. Hence the necessity for every congregation to provide families with opportunities for observing as closely as possible their child's superior human value and her joy in her religious setting. A family returning home delighted by their visit to the religious will destroy much opposition and make it easier for other families to give their own child.

4. As soon as the vocation can be put into practice, then this should be done. Twenty-one is not the canonical majority. True majority is to be judged by the standard of Christian culture and earnestness. The current opinion that it is a good thing for a girl to have known the world before entering religion seems to me to be somewhat biased. A vocation postponed is often a vocation lost. 'The Holy Spirit is the enemy of delays', affirms a seventeenth century spiritual writer. The frequently repeated assertion that 'if a girl falls down on her vocation it is because she never had one' is a fallacy which has rightly been refuted. Some of those who have subsequently married have had the courage to admit: 'We refused the call. My spiritual life has declined; it is my own fault, and I have not succeeded in reviving my husband's.'

5. Avoid sarcasm. The more influence you possess, the more any sarcastic remark of yours will be likely to put off some very sound vocations. From the lips of so many people, the girl who wishes to enter religion will hear that marriage alone is able to give true balance to a woman, and that the religious life is exceptional. A priest, speaking from experience which the candidate may imagine to be extensive, after two minutes (often no more) will rap out a too familiar 'You— a religious?' This sort of badinage from a priest is liable to kill the candidate's confidence in her vocation more certainly than the opposition of her family, however intense.

'A virgin is a gift from God, her parents' oblation, chastity's priesthood. A virgin is her mother's victim, by the daily sacrifice of which God's anger is appeased.' De Virginibus, I, 7, 32; P.L. XVI, 198.

IV   WHAT ARE THE CONDITIONS FOR THE DEVELOPMENT OF A VOCATION WHICH WAS AWAKENED AT SCHOOL

There are principally five:

1. Obedience and humility practised as much as possible at home as well as at school; passive virtues to be practised through the active virtues of devotion and creative joy.

2. Faithful adherence to the discipline of any organisation which she has parental permission to join, associating herself as closely as possible with parochial efforts; the devotion of an older Guide, a captain, or a leader of a sodality has often found its sequel in some missionary land.

3. Frequent confession to the priest responsible for following up her vocation. Even the best find it very hard to stick to the same confessor. Many have no conception at all of spiritual direction.

4. Frequent, and if possible daily communion. It would be laborious to compile the statistics showing the relationship between daily communion and faithfulness to the vocation. From my own little experience I can say that the only vocations I have seen to persevere are those of girls who were effectively committed, if not to daily communion, at any rate to observing the dictum of P. de Foucauld: 'Never miss a single communion through your own fault. . . . To receive Jesus Christ is to receive more than the universe'. The continuous and progressive growth of charity cannot be brought about without recourse to the body of our Lord; through each communion Christ widens the bounds of charity in the soul and, as Guardini says, unceasingly gives it new dimensions.

Being a religious means accepting the destruction of one's former standards, so that one is free to espouse those new bounds of charity which the Living Person of Christ proposes each day.

A letter from a girl who is now a Visitation nun is very appropriate to this subject of daily communion:

'When I made your acquaintance in 1945, I was just sixteen. For a year or two I felt slight promptings towards the religious life, but I was not always faithful in responding to this grace. I was too fond of life; there was a conflict. Then you preached us a little triduum in which you stressed the necessity for daily communion. I then made a resolution to communicate daily. The sacrifices which had to be made, and the difficulties overcome to keep my resolution, especially during the holidays, led to a rapid increase in my hunger for the Host. At the same time, perhaps because of these difficulties, I became more tenacious about receiving our Lord every day at whatever cost, and this daily gift increasingly became, to my mind, the token of a total oblation in the future, for our Lord was drawing me more and more. Yet I did succumb to the temptation of supposing that I was deluding myself, and that Christian marriage was my vocation. Then, at Holy Communion, which God gave me the grace to continue, he made me experience his divine jealousy. I could no longer say to him: "I love you with all my heart," because it seemed to be such a lie when he was wanting me for himself alone. Bit by bit, I felt the need to prolong my thanksgiving, and then to return during the day to the Tabernacle as an extension of the morning's tryst. It was through these little prayers that our Lord made me sensitive to his divine claims, and sustained me in the difficulties which had to be overcome in reaching my goal.'

This personal testimony could be corroborated by all who are acquainted with the formative value of eucharistic movements conducted with fervour (Croisade, Messagères, Cadettes).

5. Faith in the value of the vows. The vows must be thought of as a growth of real life.

It seems especially necessary to remember, above all during those moments of crisis which precede entry into religion, what could be termed the three triumphs within the three crucifixions:

'Poor, you will be rich with all the riches of God. Refusing the legitimate joys of motherhood, you will give birth to a whole multitude of children. Obedient, you will be more certain of doing your own will at its free-est, for it is no longer you yourself acting, but Jesus himself in you.'

This sums up the article which Abbot Zundel published in 1933 in La Vie Spirituelle, and which he called 'The spirit of the vows'.

6. Are there any books to help the priest to become a good diagnoser of women's vocations?

Apart from that fine book Vocation,[1] which gives an account of the first Congress, I also know of Vocations by Fr Loret (Redemptorist); Guide de l'Education d'âmes by Fr Carran, S.J. (Apostolate of Prayer); Témoins de la Cité de Dieu by Fr Carpentier, S.J.

None of the books I have read absolve priests from making a fresh effort themselves with every new vocation. One of the most painful trials for a priest faced with the question of a vocation, springs from the divergent opinions voiced about her case, not only by people of the world, but by other priests, each speaking from his own point of view.

It seems only right to remind ourselves that in many cases even minds most in harmony can differ; for example, there is the case of Angelique Arnauld (recently made famous by Montherlant), who was

[1] Vocation, Aquin Press, 1960.

refused entry to the Visitation Order by St Francis de Sales, despite the favourable verdict of Jeanne de Chantal.

7. Influence of devotional and direct evangelical Action Movements.

This is very great. I have in mind some very definite examples of great graces (sometimes even the grace of conversion) given to girls on the day of their consecration as members of the Marian societies.

The grace obtained on the day of dedication is renewed by the rules of the societies themselves, which require of their members frequent communion, daily rosary and weekly confession. This noble and difficult rule is in itself a pledge that their fervour will be maintained.

The devotional reading of Holy Scripture and of periodicals on the spiritual life seem to me to be indispensable, too.

I have learned from experience that nothing is better for a young girl than teaching the catechism to the children of the parish. Devotional movements such as Marian societies, etc., demand an apostolate which I have described as an apostolate of direct action. To be responsible for the Christian message at fourteen or fifteen, officially commits one to it for the rest of one's life.

There are the guilds and the first Friday devotions which have preserved so many vocations by snatching them from an infatuation for worldly parties and from the precocious influence of masculine society. To be a leader of a sodality requires inspiration. There are still some delusions destructive of vocations.

8. Influence of Catholic Action. Unquestionably, since 1929, the place given to marriage, in study circles even more than in preaching, has thrown much light on the grandeur of this sacrament. Yet at the present time, religious and frequently contemplative vocations seem to me to be springing up abundantly and in great numbers.

I asked a young Poor Clare: 'When did you discover that you had to enter this convent?' The novice replied: 'At a rural Congress. When I saw fifty thousand girls together, I said to myself: "What can I do to save them?" Then I thought: live a life of sacrifice for them.'

9. Can religious, teaching in those schools where vocations arise, say that they are happy about the number of girls taking the habit of their congregation after their examinations?

On this point, much work remains to be done. Here are some figures which may help to show whether the complement of vocations is decreasing or not.

We need to compare period with period, first of all, and then district with district. We could arbitrarily select four periods, beginning in 1905, the date both of the Eucharist decrees and of the expulsions: 1905–1914, 1914–1929, 1929–1945, 1945–1956.

Catholic Action commenced in 1929.

Certain houses replied to my questions, and the range of vocations chosen by senior pupils is both symptomatic and encouraging. Here are the replies from two educational houses:

Institute of Our Lady of Compiègne (House founded in 1932) (Ursulines).

From 1932–1944:
> 2 vocations: I Teaching Sister (Ursuline)
> 1 Helper of the Holy Souls

From 1944–1956: There is a marked rise in the number of vocations, thanks presumably to Catholic Action movements, Eucharistic Crusade.
> 16 vocations: 5 Teaching Sisters, 3 of which are Ursulines
> 2 Benedictines
> 1 Carmelite
> 1 Little Sister of the Assumption
> 4 Franciscans (Parochial Teachers)
> 2 Missionary Sisters
> 1 Dominican

Institute of Our Lady of Liesse (Dames de Saint-Maur).

From 1902–1914:
> 4 vocations: 3 Teaching Sisters (Saint-Maur), one of whom was a missionary foundress in Japan
> 1 Carmelite, Prioress of the Carmel at Noisy-le-Sec

No further records are available for this period, so we know only of these four. Doubtless the list is incomplete.

From 1914–1929:
> 16 vocations: 15 Teaching Sisters (Saint-Maur)
> 1 Sister of Charity

(the influence of Fr Paul de Parvillez' direction)

From 1929–1945:
> 17 vocations: 11 Teaching Sisters (Saint-Maur), two of whom were missionaries
> 2 Sisters of Charity
> 2 Franciscan Missionaries of Mary Immaculate
> 1 Sister of St Joseph de Cluny
> 1 Sister of the Holy Child Jesus de Reims

From 1945–1956:

   13 vocations: 2 Carmelites

                  11 Teaching Sisters (Saint-Maur)

If this inquiry were one day carried out, it might show that the teaching congregations are working more and more for the whole Church, and not merely for themselves (which is a gain), and also the necessity for exhaustive statements by qualified priests on the usefulness of the teaching congregations for the extension of the Kingdom of Jesus; in other words, a vast effort of voluntary propaganda is still necessary, and ought to be performed by people other than the teaching congregations themselves.

Pius XI frequently reminded us that: 'The primary charity of all is teaching,' and Pius XII, à propos of Sr Francis-Xavier Cabrini, affirmed that 'the lamentable fall of so many women who are a prey to every passion, the humiliating weakness of so many others who tremble at intimidation and derision, must be contrasted with the imperturbable and serene dignity of feminine souls morally and supernaturally strong'.

And to the pupils of the Institutes of Mother Cabrini the Pope said: 'By following the example of that admirable heroine you will learn how to put to good purpose that free time that so many others waste and dissipate in frivolous and dangerous amusements. Bright, zealous and finely tempered—it was souls like this that the Beata wished to form' (29th April, 1945).

Our priestly role is to understand and sustain courage such as this.

B. Butruille, s.j.

CHAPTER VIII

JUNIORATES AND APOSTOLIC SCHOOLS

THE PURPOSE of this short paper is to make known the result of an inquiry into that very specialised method of awakening and fostering religious vocations in girls, known as 'Juniorates' or 'Apostolic Schools' for young people.[1]

Perhaps the idea of an institution of this type gives rise to some misgivings at first. We immediately think of possible abuses; pressure on parents or children, education in a hot-house atmosphere, the danger of preparing girls who are really only 'second-rate' for the religious life.

This is too summary a judgment, which certainly has to be revised in the light of the facts.

It is almost ten years since Fr Loret, C.SS.R., now in charge of the direction of the Pontifical Organisation for Religious Vocations, and at that time already deeply interested in the problem of recruitment for women's communities, published in *Revue des Communautés Religieuses* the results of an inquiry which had brought him into touch with thirty or more French congregations having their own juniorates.[2]

In September 1952, at the first national Congress of the various federations of religious in Italy, some very conclusive reports were given by experienced directresses of these apostolic schools.

During the last few months, I myself have collected—though not in any systematic fashion—some information about twelve Juniorates. It is very striking to see how, ten years afterwards, the results predicted by Fr Loret in 1947 have in fact come to pass. Moreover, there is on all sides a great awareness of the need for this type of institution.

I shall group under various heads the most significant points. Practically, I am concerned only with French congregations.

---

[1] Although the word juniorate also indicates that stage of instruction immediately preceding the novitiate, we have thought it necessary to employ it, because it is in such common use. Undoubtedly it will be gradually replaced by the term 'apostolic school', which is in itself more expressive, and does not lead to confusion.

[2] R.C.R., 1947, p.134–138.

PLACES WHERE JUNIORATES HAVE BEEN ESTABLISHED. The greatest number are in the West. But they are also found in the East in the Lyons and Rodez region, in Haute-Savoie, and indeed in the Grand Duchy of Luxemburg and Belgium.

DATE OF FOUNDATION AND NUMBER OF PUPILS. Although a certain number of these Juniorates date back to last century, the majority of them have been founded within the last thirty years or so. Some of them receive a considerable number of children. Thus, the two Juniorates of the Daughters of the Holy Spirit (Saint-Brieuc) comprise no fewer than three hundred and twenty. Thirty or forty is an average number for well established juniorates.

METHOD OF RECRUITMENT, AND FINANCIAL SYSTEM. Usually, it is the sisters of the congregation itself who discern possible vocations in their various schools and send them on to the juniorates. Sometimes the juniorates are recommended to the best pupils at the rural schools, as boarding schools of higher education. The pupils themselves, during their holidays, will acquaint the children of their own parishes with the system. 'The example and the enthusiasm of juniorate pupils during their holidays breaks down much opposition', we are told. Families will send to the juniorate, sisters, nieces or cousins of religious. On the whole it does not appear that priests have very much to do with recruitment. But occasionally retreats and quiet days provide an opportunity for making known the work of the juniorates.

The fees are very often only half of what would be paid at an ordinary boarding school, and in any case the circumstances of the family are taken into account. To avoid any unfairness on the part of the girls or their families, those who cannot find the necessary fees are sometimes asked to pay them gradually, e.g. by teaching for a year or two later on, in the schools belonging to the Order. Alternatively, either central funds or other houses make up any deficit on the fees paid.

The minimum age for entry is eleven or twelve, and the girls stay at the juniorate until they are eighteen or nineteen.

The subjects studied are very varied, and are consistent with the capabilities of the children—some obtain their 'O' level G.C.E., and eventually prepare for the advanced level. Others, less talented, will receive some domestic or business training. Everywhere there is a real concern that the training given should equip the children for their future work in the congregation or in the world.

Similarly, the rule regarding spiritual exercises is very varied, and its provisions are not too onerous: daily Mass, sometimes not compulsory, preceded by a short meditation which may or may not be conducted; rosary in one or two cases; a visit to the Blessed Sacrament, compulsory or optional; a conference with the chaplain, and confession every fortnight; an annual retreat and one or more days of recollection. On Sundays, assistance at High Mass and Vespers with the community. Membership of particular groups or sodalities completes their spiritual training.

EXTERNAL CONTACTS. In all cases, the pupils go home for their holidays, as at other boarding schools. A particular Juniorate may re-assemble its pupils in the middle of the summer vacation for a fortnight in camp or on holiday.

Those who are taking courses at other schools are obviously in daily contact with young people of their own age.

Frequently, some time in a school is required between the end of their Juniorate days and the beginning of their postulancy.

OBJECTIONS. It must not be thought that directresses of Juniorates or the chaplains are unaware of the dangers of this institution. One superior writes:

'It is clear that we must be alive to the dangers, shared by all boarding schools, which "living-in" presents. Among these dangers we note—a relatively easy life, the temptation to be wrapped up in oneself, and a consequent lack of responsibility and of contact with the suffering and unhappiness of others, the danger of an insufficiently virile and aggressive atmosphere, the danger of routine in the spiritual life and of a gregarious mentality which is detrimental to the development of personality.'

But this same superior indicates many methods which are adopted to remedy these disadvantages: a knowledge, adapted to the pupil's age, of the problems confronting religion at the present day (biblical conferences with film-strips, the Church of Silence), missionary and social problems (the homeless, etc.); a desire for real culture through literature, music, the cinema; a sense of responsibility (no supervision of study or of dormitories), the organisation of social functions, economies to help maintain a poor seminarist.

RESULTS. Broadly speaking, the number of vocations coming from the juniorate represents a very high percentage; in a large congregation it has been as high as 50 per cent some years; now, because the children enter younger and are less clear about their vocation, the proportion is lower because some of them leave. But about 40–45 per cent stay.

Another congregation, which gives a figure of 40 per cent vocations, notes that the standard of perseverance of former juniorate pupils, especially after temporary vows, is higher than that of their companions coming directly from the world.

In other cases the ratio between admissions to the juniorate and entry into postulancy is in the region of 25–30 per cent.

More important than the figures perhaps, these statements, coming from so many different quarters, do show that the juniorate is a very timely method of awakening, fostering and preserving some excellent vocations:

'In the circumstances from which our candidates come, it seems to me that the juniorates are the only means of ensuring that they reach the postulant stage initiated and prepared, both from the intellectual and moral points of view. Of course, there will certainly be well-instructed candidates who will enter the novitiate without passing through the juniorate, and it is to be hoped that their numbers will increase; but without the juniorate the majority of our children will have received almost no training, as such, at all. How many timid and hesitant souls, in other surroundings, must have lost an embryo vocation, fragile, perhaps, but of good quality.

In areas such as our rural parishes in Brittany, still traditionally Christian, but attacked by those harmful influences which are spreading everywhere, the juniorate seems to be the ideal method of realising, fostering and preserving some excellent vocations which would certainly have been lost if they had had to wait for the normal age for entry into postulancy.

In the case of vocations among town children, it is easy to see that the juniorate is even more necessary. Yet because of their prejudices against this form of education, which is too disciplined for their liking, it is difficult to recruit pupils from among them. Parents, for their part, are openly opposed to it, because they consider the Christian education given in our local schools sufficient.'

THE ROLE OF THE CHAPLAIN. It is hardly necessary to note, in conclusion, the importance of the priest's work in the smooth running of the juniorate. Whether it be the sound and progressive teaching of religion, initiation into mental prayer, instruction in the liturgy, facility in confession, patient and prudent spiritual direction, eventual visits to the girls' families to obtain a better understanding of their home background, the priest has a vital part to play. Though often hidden, this ministry has its fruits in the growth of some fine religious vocations, and one who realises its full worth cannot fail to be a convinced partisan of the juniorates, when conducted wisely and with an equal concern for both human and spiritual education.

Did not the Church pronounce long ago on the value of Junior Seminaries as nurseries of vocations to the priesthood (c. 1354)? The system has been adopted by many orders and congregations of men. Why should not this be usefully done for women's vocations to the religious life? The experiments which have been made, and the acute sense that superiors always have of their responsibilities, will enable them to avoid the perils of this enterprise, and lead safely to port those young girls who, without it, would neither have been conscious of our Lord's call, nor prepared to respond to it.

E. BERGH, S.J.
Director of *La Revue des Communautés Religieuses.*

CHAPTER IX

THE PRIEST'S ROLE IN AWAKENING VOCATIONS IN HIS PARISH AND IN THE HOME

THERE IS no point in trying to show that the role of a parish priest, whether rector or curate, is of fundamental and essential importance in awakening religious vocations. This is quite clear from facts known to us all: a new priest arrives in the parish, and as soon as he has had time to exercise his pastoral ministry to any effect, some young girls will begin to contemplate the novitiate, and there will be a movement towards the religious life, something quite new or at any rate possessing a breadth unknown before his time. Then he leaves the parish for some new post, and the spring dries up, or rather this priest seems to have taken it away with him. They will say that he has a 'charisma', as if this 'charisma' were a personal thing, and had no connection with his priesthood, or with priesthood at all. Pius XII tells us, in the words of St Ambrose, that 'It has ever been typical of priestly grace to sow the seeds of chastity and to kindle devotion to virginity'.[1]

It is easy to understand why the rector of a parish should possess this power. More than any one else, he is aware of those social factors which exercise such a powerful influence on a vocation: the atmosphere of the home and work, the girl's past life and family background. More than any one else he is in a position to influence the conditions which affect the growth and development of a girl's aspiration to make the total sacrifice.

How is the priest to apply this power, which the Lord has placed in his hands, to the awakening of vocations in the parish and in the home?

His function is twofold—to create a climate favourable to the awakening of vocations, and to work for them.

---

[1] Encyc: *Sacra Virginitas*, C.T.S. p. 25.

I To Create a Climate Favourable to the Awakening of Vocations

A. The Priest Himself.

The priest himself is the prime factor in creating the right climate of opinion.

Pierre le Frontalier, in *Prêtre et Apôtre* for 15th November, 1950, cites in these words the reaction of one curate:

'Some young girls acquaint him of their imminent entry into a local congregation. The curate explodes! "These days, we do not need good Sisters, but Christian homes; it will be through Christian homes that our country will be regenerated, re-Christianised; to enter religion would be a mistake, a great mistake; marriage is a duty, the supreme duty".'

We must not attach too much importance to such extravagances. But Pope Pius XII was not speaking idly when he addressed himself to 'those priests, laymen, preachers, orators or writers who have not a word of approval or praise for virginity dedicated to Christ; who, for some years now, despite the warnings of the Church and contrary to her mind, have conceded to marriage a fundamental superiority over virginity; who go even so far as to present it as the only means capable of ensuring the development and natural fulfilment of human personality' (Allocution of 15th September, 1952). Nor was he speaking idly when, in the Encyclical *Sacra Virginitas*, he denounced this same opinion as a 'dangerous error'.[1] Nor were the Cardinals and Archbishops speaking without due consideration when they requested the clergy to

'mitigate the consequences of an extravagant and unskilful propaganda on behalf of the lawful spirituality of Christian marriage'.

There is certainly no question of minimising the importance of the sacrament of marriage. To have a deeper appreciation of its rich possibilities for sanctification is one of the graces of our age. There is no question of minimising the importance of Catholic Action. Naturally, we can have no more than a glimpse of the part it will be called on to play in the future evangelisation of the world. But it is one of the weaknesses of the human mind to fluctuate between two extremes. In this, as in other matters, reaction tends to go too far, and to swing beyond the point of balance. It is easy enough to disparage the religious life in order to enhance marriage, to belittle the apostolate of the religious in order to give more prominence to that of the laity.

The priest, more than most, will be tempted to do this, when, after a long struggle, he has managed to find among the lifeless mass one invaluable lay person on whom the whole movement seems to depend

[1] Encyc: *Sacra Virginitas*, C.T.S. p. 23.

—his hope of a really Christian home, which is the main factor in the regeneration of his parish.

The evidence of novices and young nuns is too weighty and concordant for us not to credit it. Even then we have only heard from those who have surmounted the difficulty. There must be many who have understood priests to mean that they would do more good by remaining in the world; that by entering an Order they would stifle their rich potentialities in narrowness, in antiquated and out-moded customs—this, to the youth of today, is an almost irresistible argument. There is no question of formal opposition; it is an attitude which can be described in the word incomprehension, and a consequently poor opinion, when it is not a wrong opinion.

Many people smile at the nuns' failings. They are anxious to have their services, but they are not anxious to help them, either by raising their spiritual and apostolic stature or by stimulating recruitment to their ranks. And so long as the priest lacks understanding, there is no point in speaking of his role in the awakening of vocations, for he is all for extinguishing them.

To give, one must have. Before having, one must be. There can be neither light nor heat without the hearth. This understanding, this esteem, this love of consecrated virginity, which the priest has to encourage in his parish and in its Christian homes, must first be his own vital and contagious conviction.

Fundamental convictions:

1. For a young girl, a religious vocation is in itself the greatest, most beautiful, devoted and beneficent of lives, not only because it offers the most favourable conditions for personal sanctification, but also because of its very nature it normally makes possible the greatest, most beautiful and most complete service of God and men.

2. The parish needs the religious life, not only because it puts chosen workers into every sector of spiritual and corporal charity, but, at a deeper level, because it is a public state of perfection within the Church.

The religious state is a living example to all the baptised of a total response to the claims of baptism; to all members of the Church, of the perfect ecclesial community; to all Christians, who must tend towards the perfection of love and cannot do so without entering into the spirit of the counsels, and their effective and communal practice.

'Dead indeed to sin, but alive to God'—the Christian must reckon himself thus. It helps and strengthens him to have before his very eyes the complete renuniciation of the egoisms of possessions, of pleasure and of independence, those three great dominions of sin, and also the total offering of hearts and lives to God.

The observance of the counsels works like an active and powerful ferment in society. He who is detached from all things helps him who keeps his goods to remain free, despite his possessions. Held in thrall by a sexual nature wounded by original sin, would people think of marriage in a Christian fashion, would they live their married life as Christians, without the shining and attractive ideal of perfect chastity?

In leading his people to sanctity, what a help it is to the priest to be able to point to the public practice of 'sanctification, and of effective and adequate measures towards its attainment'.[1]

3. The community of the parish must provide children for the religious life. If its members are really anxious to imitate Christ, then there will necessarily be some who will want to follow him the whole way.

The aspiration to perfection, without which there can be no Christian fervour in the parish, will make at any rate a few souls sensitive to the appeal: 'If thou wouldst be perfect'. The essential test of a parish's Christianity is in the children it gives to the state of perfection.

4. Pius XII said: 'The general apostolate of the Church, at the present time would be almost inconceivable without the co-operation of religious. While, in the Christian world and indeed beyond it, appeals for Catholic sisters are heard today more than ever before, we see them forced regretfully to refuse one after another; sometimes they are even compelled to abandon their former good works, such as hospitals and educational establishments, all because vocations are insufficient to meet the needs' (Discourse of 15th September, 1952).

We are well placed, in France, for appreciating what havoc is caused through lack of religious. To mention but one of the more serious examples, the number of Seminaries closing their doors for want of pupils is increasing. When we look for explanations for this dwindling in the numbers of candidates for the priesthood, we discover that one of the most certain causes is the progressive closing of girls' schools since the beginning of the century, not for want of pupils or lack of

[1] Encyc: *Provida Mater Ecclesia*, D.C. 1947, col. 579.

resources, but for lack of religious to run them. So long as the hearts of future mothers were formed by religious at Christian schools, there were found homes sufficiently Christian to understand and sustain a vocation. Nowadays, they are simply not there. And so with each generation we sink more deeply into the mire.

In this grave crisis, no possible vocation should go unfostered. And every priest should look at the problem with a catholic eye. The Christian priest, feeling himself entrusted with the riches which can save all, will want to help the largely de-christianised areas to find the religious which they need. The priest, whose land is really too poor to be able, in the normal course, to produce vocations in the immediate future, will, through Catholic Action, prepare homes in which they will soon blossom.

'The need for vocations to virginity is immense, and we cannot believe that Christ does not impart to youthful hearts their full share of grace. It is we who are failing that grace . . .' (Fr Carpentier, S.J.).

5. The call to the religious life is of compelling urgency in the world of today. This restless world cannot find stability because it is wanting in love.

Now, by dispersing those egoisms which are radically opposed to the unity required by the Mystical Body, the three Counsels are directed as much towards fraternal love and the rebuilding of the human family in Christ as towards a personal love for our heavenly Father. The religious life actively maintains the evangelical social order in the Church; it is the realisation of the highest form of community according to the mind of the Mystical Body; it is an appeal to all Christians in their diverse earthly circumstances; it is an ideal which stimulates and directs their efforts towards the unity of the human family. The religious speaks to the world of the depths of its disunity and of the indispensable condition for the new brotherhood, i.e. victory over all egoisms.

6. *In manibus tuis sortes meae:* to the priest the whole Church is entrusted; but within the Church the state of perfection comes first. *Illustrior pars gregis Christi:* how can the priest not share Christ's own predilection for these chosen ones of the flock who are entrusted so completely to his care?

It is up to the priest to be the soul of that vital spirit manifested by the Christian community in the young people it gives to the state of perfection.

Never does his ministry more effectively serve the faithful, his parish and the Church, than when he leads a soul through religious profession to the perfect ecclesial community.

Nil volitum quin praecognitum. It is unlikely that the clergy will hold these basic convictions with any tenacity if teaching on the religious state and its eminent dignity in the Church is not given at the Seminary; not merely a few conferences outside the syllabus, which are given only superficial consideration, but as a subject for study and examination. A teaching which will, with experience, beget esteem and love, and which provides a detailed understanding of the theological and psychological criteria of vocation, without which, through fear of venturing into unknown territory, the priest will refrain altogether—or make mistakes which will dishearten him.

B. THE OUTLOOK OF THE PARISH

How will the priest communicate these basic convictions to the people of his parish?

1. *By his own prayer* and the prayers which he will encourage his people to offer for religious vocations.

Before being the free response of the person called, a vocation is the choice of divine predilection. And that vision, which is so lacking in the world today, of the excellence of consecrated virginity is primarily the gift of God.

Many parishes have organised and maintained a wave of prayer for vocations to the priesthood. The primary concern of the priest who wishes to create the right climate of opinion will be to make prayer for religious vocations a habit among Christians.

2. *By his own attitude.* The priest should always speak with special esteem and constant sympathy of religious in general, and those of his own parish in particular.

He must take great care to sustain them, to encourage them in their spiritual life and apostolic activity—confession, direction, doctrinal, scriptural and liturgical instruction and help them by every means in his power to find their place in the apostolic work of the parish.

Not only will religious gain in prestige as a result, but, within the bounds of the parish, where everyone knows everyone else, this deep and constant interest of the pastor will, more than any words, inspire respect, esteem and love for the religious life.

3. *By his teaching.*

(a) When he is catechising, preaching, giving spiritual direction or writing his parish magazine, the priest must not be limited to those minimum obligations which he will observe in giving 'lenient' absolutions. His teaching should re-echo the sweeping appeals of the Gospel, so that many will at any rate embrace their spirit, and those who are still free to do so will desire, if it is God's will, to put them into practice. In this way, he will help the birth of numerous vocations, both priestly and religious.

To preach the counsels, it is sufficient to pass on the message exactly as it is. On almost every page, true evangelical perfection, if not demanded, is at least recommended as the normal fulfilment of aspiration for those who wish to follow Christ. When we look at the early Christian communities, it is obvious that the apostles first preached the Jesus they had known, and the way of life they had lived with him, the 'apostolic' life, nostalgia for which causes the state of perfection to be continually reborn in the Church. The aspiration to the imitation of Christ inspired its precepts. The spirit of the counsels was everywhere. Today, only this spirit will still be a leaven powerful enough to renew our parishes, to raise up not only priests, monks and nuns, but also laity with sufficient generosity to live fully Catholic lives.

(b) One way for the priest to uphold the religious life in his preaching is to give full emphasis to true evangelical perfection. A second way is to point out the full breadth of its apostolic and missionary effects.

It is a fact that many are drawn both to the religious life and to the secular priesthood by the great idea of the growth of the Mystical Body. The grace of vocation is often embodied in an acute awareness of some apostolic task. Young people particularly need the appeal of a great mission in their lives, but familiarity often blinds them to the tremendous tasks which are before their very eyes.

Nor need we be afraid that our own diocese, our own land, will be deprived of the resources of which they stand in so much need. A vocation born under the influence of missionary enthusiasm frequently develops in a different direction which proves to be more suited to the candidate's health, aptitudes and inclinations, and to the Church's need. It is indeed the Gospel, the universal Church, which we have to preach. The more zeal there is for missionary work, the more apostles we shall obtain for every task, and the higher their quality will be.

Such emphasis is particularly necessary because this point of view is almost unrepresented in the older catechisms and it has hardly yet penetrated even to the new manuals of religious teaching. Only in the most modern editions is it stressed that catholicity is not only a mark of the true Church, but is vitally necessary for its expansion. The devil is quick to seize on such omissions. If communism has roused the enthusiasm of the young for the liberation of the world, is it not in part because such a world-wide outlook has been absent from our own teaching, because we have not repeated often enough that Christ is the only hope of the whole world?

(c) It is of supreme importance, throughout the presentation of the Gospel message, to glorify the state of perfection, to make men sensitive to the appeal of the religious ideal. Some positive teaching will be possible in the climate thus created, and though it is not for me to go into detail it will stem mainly from two points:

(i) The nature of the religious life and the place and function of the state of perfection within the Church.

(ii) A true idea of vocation.

Such extensive preaching of the counsels can take more than one form: e.g. pictures can be displayed of religious from the parish, and the work they are doing; special celebrations can be held for the jubilee of a religious loved for her devotion; articles in the parish magazine can encourage the faithful to be proud of the numerous vocations, or to aspire, as they should, to foster more. These are just a few of the many ways in which the teaching given in catechism and sermons can be amplified.

C. THE OUTLOOK OF THE HOME

Reading the evidence collected in *Risquer sa vie pour Dieu* we cannot fail to be struck by the number of girls who have had to overcome opposition from their families before being able to respond to the call.

Obviously such vocations, opposed from the start, are particularly spectacular, and attract a certain publicity and this may in part explain why there is such a high proportion of them in this collection. It is nevertheless true that family objections, which are common enough when a son thinks of the priesthood, arise much more frequently when a daughter contemplates the religious life. It is futile to expect the body of religious which the Church and the world need, to come from homes with such an outlook.

In talking to Christian parents about the evangelical state of perfection and its place in the Church as a whole, the priest must lead them to think of a religious vocation not only as the highest solution to the problem of their daughter's future, but rather as the best possible fulfilment of their family. Their marriage cannot be lived in its Christian fulness unless they accept the orientations implicit in the sacrament, a turning to Christ, to Mary, towards virginal love, which 'instead of following the practice of marriage, aspires to that which it symbolises' (Roman Pontifical, 'Of the Consecration of Virgins'). Christian parents, who are responsible for continuing, through their children, the secular effort of the members of Christ towards the perfection of charity, will want to give a son or a daughter to the ideal of Virginity. In this child of theirs their whole line attains the highest end of its progress, the plenary love of Christ. 'Consecrated souls, emanating from the human family, are as it were the terminal flower in which the whole of creation attains the fulness of its collective destiny.'[1]

Parents, inspired by such motives, must be given a proper understanding of vocation if we are going to avoid disastrous blunders. There are those who, regarding the field of 'vocation' as pertaining to God alone, his own imperious call, an irresistible attraction, think they are not required to assist the action of grace, but rather to put obstacles in its way in order to try it. And there are others who, seeing vocation as a matter concerning the soul and God alone, feel that they must maintain an oppressive silence or a paralysing neutrality.

Not that parents ought to be advised to exercise any sort of positive pressure. This would in any case most likely evoke a stubborn refusal, particularly in the case of young people who express their personality by opposing any pressure which they resent. The danger inherent in a morally forced acceptance would be even graver; since when she later reaches maturity the religious may experience violent temptations against the life she has chosen.

The parents' real co-operation consists in desiring vocations in their home, in voicing this desire to God in prayer, and in not being afraid to express it, with tact and discretion, in front of the children. By their remarks to all their children, and a more personal word to one in particular, they can encourage them to question themselves before God about the choice of their state of life. Girls as well as boys ought

[1] Canon Hoornaert, Essence et beauté de la vie religieuse in *Recrutement sacerdotal*, April 1952, p. 103.

to know that among the prospects for their future envisaged by parents there is possibly the supreme total gift of their hearts and lives to God.

'There are good books', observes Fr Carpentier, 'to facilitate that initiation of children into life, which is normally incumbent on the parents. It is surprising that Catholic authors go into marriage in considerable detail, without putting the ideal of virginity forward at all. Yet Christ, and our Lady the ideal of perfect chastity—always visible in the Church—are there to help them to do this. It seems inadmissible that the time when they are receiving a revelation of life which perhaps makes too great an impression on them, their thoughts are directed only towards the foundation of a home, without mentioning, with all the necessary reserve, the possibility of an eventual vocation, when the Lord has already inspired them with a desire for it. Is this acting in conformity with the Gospel? Does it not deprive these young people, at a most critical time, of that succour foreseen in the Redemption, the virginal beauty of Jesus and Mary? Does this not overthrow for ever in the minds which are being formed, the true scale of Christian values? Does it not do a grave wrong, not only to the young people themselves, but also to the Kingdom of God, to the Church and to those innumerable souls who are looking for just this?'[1]

Please God this profound Christian realism will be understood by all those who have to perform 'this initiation into life', and by all those authors who deal with this subject.

The co-operation which God expects of parents in the awakening of vocations, consists not only of words, which can be very clumsy, but also of deeds. They have to create a whole climate of faith, poverty, charity, devotion, courage and joy. This is directly opposed to the egoism of those who practise birth-control because they only want one boy and one girl, an egoism which necessarily fashions the whole outlook of the children towards purely earthly success. The atmosphere of the Christian home will be the very opposite; it will be a happy, generous, unselfish, universal, apostolic and missionary atmosphere; the ambition will be not to 'have more' but to 'be more', not to 'succeed' but to 'serve'; in short, an atmosphere in which the child, already breathing the spirit of the counsels, will find himself well on the way to loving and choosing their effective realisation.

II AWAKENING RELIGIOUS VOCATIONS

The outlook of the family and of the parish just described will give souls freedom to respond to the appeal of the Spirit, which will often move them without the assistance of any intermediary. But not always,

[1] *Note doctrinale sur la vocation religieuse*, Edit. du C.D.S., Tournai, Belgium.

however. There are girls, though not perhaps so many as boys, who are unaware that they have a vocation, and the priest must help them to become conscious of it.

Here, the essential role passes to the spiritual director, whose function, as well as the theological and psychological criteria for discerning vocations, has been discussed in earlier chapters.

It only remains for me to point out some of the fields in which the parish priest might interfere with the work of the director.

A. PREPARATION

Since we must only speak about vocations in a personal way to those who are prepared for it, the priest's job, in his parochial organisations for girls, is to make plain the way of the Lord.

(a) Remote Preparation

This will cover all those preliminaries, without which the call of God cannot be understood and followed.

(i) The sense of evangelical abnegation. The principal difficulty modern girls meet in the religious life is the necessity for persevering in obscure effort. Spurts of generosity are there, but too often they rest on transient feelings which the religious must learn to discipline. The religious life consists in a long and constant effort in sacrifice, joyful certainly, but envisaged clearly and accepted freely, with all the mortifications of nature that this implies. It is necessary to make young people see that real generosity is not occasional bursts of enthusiasm, but a free and courageous correspondence with grace by an adult person, who has weighed and accepted the fact that she will have to struggle against the vagaries of emotion. Young people must be taught as soon as they begin to grow up, not to despise their feelings but to master them.

(ii) The sense of God. Less should be said about the development of personality and more about self-effacement, and about losing oneself in union and conformity with the unique and transcendent personality of Christ Jesus. Only thus will a young girl be able to understand the incomparable value of total consecration to God, for in the case of a religious, consecration surpasses devotion, since her devotion flows from her consecration.

(iii) An apostolic and missionary sense which is centred on God rather than on persons; those for whom their neighbour is the principal Christian reality, and God the second, are temperamentally unsuited to the religious life.

(b) Immediate Preparation

(i) This will aim at making people see that the state of perfection is a supremely desirable good: e.g. group teaching on the state of perfection, which will find its place in a more general survey of the various states of life.

Susceptibilities must be respected, and future mothers of families can be reached by broadening the discussion. In general it can be on the lines that France, the world and the Church are short of religious.

What girls can do about it—offer themselves for the religious life; influence of parents, friends and companions on a vocation; vocations in the homes of the future.

(ii) Great care must be taken to dispel widespread but false notions about vocation, which deceive many young people into giving no further thought to the matter beyond 'That does not concern me, it's not my problem'. A true idea of vocation often leads them to recognise that for them the question does arise, and even to discover signs, hitherto undecipherable, of the divine call in themselves.

Exactly the same false ideas must be dispelled in the case of girls as His Excellency Mgr Duperray denounces in respect of vocations to the priesthood:[1]

A too sentimental conception: 'Do I feel emotionally attracted to the religious life?', rather than one based on reason: 'Do I "will" to be a religious?' Christ said to the rich young man: 'Wilt thou?', not 'Do you feel inclined to follow me?'

This is valid for girls too, bearing in mind, of course, their psychological make-up and the fact that they are moved less by principles than by emotions and impressions.

A too passive conception: 'The question, so far as the child is concerned, is not so much to know whether God is calling him, as to know whether he wills to give himself to God; instead of waiting, it behoves him to offer himself'.

This echoes Louis Sempé's reminder:

'Vocation, if it is genuine, is indeed the word of God, but a word which, when it finds an echo in the soul, there takes on the forms of human thought and follows the laws of our psychology . . . in the majority of cases vocation then appears as the choosing of a human career, except that its motives are of a supernatural order.'[2]

A too individualistic conception: 'Do I feel inclined to be a

---

[1] *Vers un plus grand amour*, pp. 182–3.
[2] Art. 'Vocation' in *Dict. Theol. Cath.*, col. 3. 178.

religious?', instead of considering what God is expecting of them and
the needs of souls and of the world: 'Is Christ, are men, waiting for me?
Where can I serve them best?'

B. The Great Occasions for Awakening Vocations

To awaken desire for the religious life, Providence uses the most
varied and often the most unexpected means. There are, however,
some occasions which are particular propitious for the action of grace.

(a) Most important are *retreats*. It is a fact of experience that many
vocations are awakened or decided on during a retreat. The priest
should therefore encourage girls to go into enclosed retreat, and
should organise parochial or group retreats for them. In these retreats,
religious vocation should be brought well to the fore, and not kept in
the background or left out altogether, as too often happens. Naturally,
possible aspirants are in a minority. But how can they be reached
except through the group? And is there not some urgency to present
the others with these truths if we want them, later on, to create a
favourable atmosphere in their own homes?

(b) Parochial or deanery 'Vocation days' have the advantage of
reaching both the young girl and her neighbourhood, and familiarising
them with the idea.

They are a normal way of putting the question to boys and young
men. It is a matter of urgency that they should similarly be used for
bringing the question of religious vocation before older and younger
girls.

Concerning the younger girls, nearly all the inquiries conducted
lately among priests and religious show that many of them trace the
origin of their vocation to a very tender age. The Church, in her Code
of Law, lays down that priests, especially rectors and curates, should
bestow particular solicitude on children who show signs of an ecclesiastical vocation, and should foster in them the germ of divine vocation.

It is the same Spirit who moves both men and women to the generosity of the total oblation, and, while bearing in mind differences of
temperament, we ought to foster the germs of vocation in younger
girls as well as boys.

It is clear that any choice made by children will have to be ratified
after adolescence if it is to be fully valid. But since it is impossible at
first to pick out those who are answering a divine call, we must treat
them all with the same respect. That contempt for children's vocations

shown nowadays by so many laymen, and even priests, is opposed to the mind of the Church and of Christ; and undoubtedly, in many cases, it is a selfish pride which makes it impossible for them to conceive any other way to God except the one by which they themselves were drawn. Let us not pretend that we can circumscribe the Spirit in the unfathomable variety of his way. Let us carefully foster adult vocations. But let us pay more attention than ever to children's vocations. We need both so much if the gap is to be bridged.

A reminder about total self-offering to God will not be inopportune when the children are preparing for their Communions. It ought never to be omitted at retreats before solemn Communion or the Profession of faith. Enclosed retreats for the pick of the younger girls, as well as for boys, are to be encouraged.

Retreats, Vocations days, with talks suitably arranged, are privileged opportunities for awakening vocations, but they are exceptional and transient. One excellent way of following up and perpetuating their helpful influence—or, where necessary, as a substitute for them—is to provide a section of well-chosen books on religious vocation for the parochial or guild library.

C. THE PRIEST AND THE HOME

The final, and delicate, question.

First of all, let us recognise that valid reasons do exist for delaying entry into the novitiate, and that Christian parents are sometimes better judges of these than ourselves. It may be that 'priests have no real knowledge of the girls they send. They see them at work in charitable organisations, i.e. in their contacts with the outside world, but often they have not the slightest idea of the attitude and disposition they reveal when they are at home with their families, whereas it is chiefly in their family life that people show themselves for what they are.'[1] We shall therefore listen to these reasons, and take into consideration those which throw doubt on the reality of a vocation.

On the other hand, the priest will often have to intervene, with tact and prudence, but with an evangelical confidence to dispel prejudices and overcome hesitancy. Many parents think their children have been influenced or carried away by passing fancies. Often they are afraid, understanding nothing of the boldness of grace. They must be told that postulancy and the novitiate will be a genuine test of the vocation,

Vocation, Aquin Press, 1960. p. 72.

but under conditions best fitted to strengthen and preserve it. Admission into postulancy is usually the best method for verifying the call, vocation being a very high favour which one must endeavour to preserve.

When there is parental opposition the priest must affirm the transcendence of the divine call, sustain the candidate's courage, and make her wait patiently. I shall not dwell on those vocations which are actually unfulfilled because the child has a duty to assist her parents in their grave need. If the obstacle is nothing more than the parents' arbitrary will, the child has certainly the right to decide her own life, but it is not always expedient for her to exercise it. The director must not push matters imprudently to an open break, if that would mean her infringing the civil law, or if it would leave her without resources if, later on, she had to cut short her novitiate through lack of vocation. He can only pray that he may see the matter clearly, and know whether to wait or to act, following the grand example left us by some of the saints. The evidence collected in *Risquer sa vie pour Dieu* shows that frequently parents who did not give their consent at first have gradually acquiesced in their daughter's vocation, perceiving that in it she finds her fulfilment and her joy.

The crisis in religious vocations in France is too grave to be solved by the efforts of a few propagandists, or by the solicitude of religious alone. The desired outlook can only be created by the concerted action of all, in particular through the co-operation of the secular clergy, and especially of priests in parishes.

In the light of certain experiments in various quarters, it can be stated categorically that if all priests made up their minds to make the effort which is in their power, the number of religious in France could easily be doubled. Then many problems of evangelisation, today insoluble, could easily be solved.

CANON ARNAUD,
Associate Director of C.D.S.

CHAPTER X

THE PRIEST AND VOCATIONS IN SPECIALISED CATHOLIC ACTION GROUPS

First, some preliminary remarks by way of introduction:

1. The priestly ministry of the chaplain to some specialised Catholic Action group is part of an integral whole—the apostolic training given by a particular movement, which is a movement of laymen. The priest's work is fundamental yet discreet. It has more in common with the assistance given by an educator than with the contribution of a teacher or director. His influence is therefore in one way inseparable from that of the movement itself, and is closely associated with the findings, the demands and the difficulties of a specialised work of Catholic Action.

We shall soon see that, far from being minimised, his role is thus thrown into peculiar relief, provided we are prepared to appreciate the place of specialised Catholic Action in the apostolic life of the laity.

2. We propose to deal only with the role of the priesthood in general, and not of any particular priest. One of the striking things in the various statements we have received is, in fact, the emphasis placed on contacts made, thanks to the movement, with the priests who are chaplains at the various levels. The result, has been a deeper appreciation of priesthood itself, which has had profound consequences on every single vocation.

3. And lastly, so that the value of our remarks can be truthfully assessed here are the sources of our information:

(a) Statements by religious received via those movements to which they formally belonged.

(b) Articles that have appeared in *Masses Ouvrières*.

(c) An interview with four religious in the same house, who formerly belonged to four different movements.

(d) Comparison of the practical experiences of the two writers of this article, one in an independent society, the other among the working classes.

Our account will be in two parts:

I. Specialised Catholic Action and the Religious Life.

II. The role of the priest in awakening and sustaining vocations.

I   SPECIALISED CATHOLIC ACTION AND THE RELIGIOUS LIFE

In a sense, as we have said, the priest's ministry is dependent on the apostolic aim of the specialised Catholic Action movement. It is therefore necessary to get clear at once the fundamental points on which this ministry will have to rely.

1. CONTRIBUTIONS

(a) One of the principal notes characteristic of the requirements of specialised Catholic Action, which seems to have a profound influence in awakening religious vocations, is the necessity for living one's whole life in the light of the Gospel.

People are continually being put off by what the jargon of Catholic Action calls the 'two compartments': side by side with a certain amount of Christian living (practice, and personal faith) there is one's everyday life, which seems to be immersed in paganism or in a de-Christianised mentality.

To quote a case in point:

'The first discovery I made at J.E.C. was that I had to be a Christian twenty-four hours a day. It brought home to me that the whole of life must be given to Christ. One feels geared to the activity; that one must give a blank cheque to God. By telling a priest at a Catholic Action meeting my various problems in all their littleness, I learnt that to the Lord nothing is irrelevant or profane. When I first began my apostolic work, I used to wonder why a priest should interest himself in the way a girl passed her Sundays or spent her money.'

We know the answer well enough—because God is interested in these things; because our actual life as men and women is as it were the raw material for our Christian life, the privileged field in which it is to be exercised, making, as it does, heavy demands on our faith, our hope and our charity.

This fearless realism of Christianity, which is unceasingly stressed and reaffirmed in the aims of Catholic Action, bears within itself as it were a hidden appeal to the undivided oblation. It is interesting to observe that it is often revealed to the members through the chaplain's humble and ready attention to what they have to say about their homes, their work and their spare time. Through the chaplain's interest in the

things that make up their lives, many members have seen, without
having it pointed out to them, that God himself is interested in human
realities, and that these things must be re-examined in the light of
the faith, and re-lived in the spirit of the evangelical Beatitudes. They
have realised the need to examine their way of doing things, of
acting, living and thinking; to discover at every turn what God
thinks, to bring every single human reality under the influence of
the faith.

It is easy to see what an important place the chaplain holds in this
education in the faith—education in the realism of the faith.

A former militant, now a religious, has written:

'By constantly urging me to look at everything with the eye of faith, from
the Lord's point of view, the priest helped me to bridge the gap between the
faith of my childhood and adult faith; to strip me of a sentimental faith so that
I might acquire living faith.'

(b) Another fundamental point maintains the aims of specialised
Catholic Action and constitutes a powerful factor in education for the
apostolate. It is the acceptance of that supernatural solidarity which
binds us to others, in grace as well as in sin. A sense of, and a concern
for, others—for our brethren whom Christ wishes to love and to save
through us.

'I discovered the true meaning of Christian charity to my neighbour. J.O.C.
asked me to attend a conference of officials. . . . I then understood my responsibility—it ought not to be my own personality, but Christ himself, that I
had to pass on to others; and these others possessed Christ, albeit secretly. From
that day my love for others was more real and was my only reason for living;
my enthusiasm for others was transformed into enthusiasm for God.'

It has been the school of total oblation for many.

'From that time I tried to live the present moment, to forget myself, to give
myself to others more. I went to Mass every day to tell the Lord of my love
and to place upon the paten the suffering which was all around me and which
tore my heart as if I were personally responsible for it.'

Or again:

'I felt the weight of the anxieties of others so keenly that all the difficulties
at the office seemed trifling, and everything in my life turned to Christ.'

(c) Catholic Action has encouraged men to enter more personally
into the mystery of redemption, which bids us ransom the society in
which the Providence of God has placed us, and has, in addition,
brought a living discovery of the living Christ to many.

'It was J.A.C.F. which first introduced me to holy Scripture, and particularly
the Gospel. Our Lord became a living person, closer to me. Christianity was no
longer merely the religion in which I had always lived, and which appeared

to be a life of routine and prohibitions. A personal choice had to be made, and I had to live in accordance with this choice.'

Catholic Action has been the means of a living discovery of the living Christ pursuing his work today, his work in the Church.

'We knew that our work was a work of the Church, in which we co-operated with the hierarchy in a movement controlled by it.'

And again:

'For me, the characteristic contribution of Catholic Action was the discovery of the dimensions of the Mystical Body, and an incessant solicitude for its fulfilment. . . . Catholic Action is engaged in the service of the Church for the evangelisation of the world.'

There is also the realism of its faith, a redemptive solidarity, a sense of belonging to Christ in the Church. Such is, very briefly, the positive contribution of specialised Catholic Action in the Christian and apostolic, and hence, religious, education of Christians.

2. DIFFICULTIES

But there is no light without shadow. The training received in the various movements does not of itself remove certain ambiguities or limitations which may well prove to be obstacles in the way of God's call to the religious life. But these very uncertainties and limitations are not without use, since they help us to define still more clearly the place and role of the priest. It is hardly surprising if these apostolic enterprises, especially in the case of young people, are accompanied by inadequacy or excess; the weight of sin works its way into the most generous pursuits.

(a) We will give several instances: a sense of the Church, a vital discovery of the Mystical Body. For many, doubtless, particularly among the working class, this positive and vital perception is mingled with a difficulty in accepting the visible Church, and in feeling a sense of solidarity with and dependence on it.

'In the J.O.C. we adopted the attitude of the workers, who react very strongly against authority. . . . The result was a natural and unthinking antipathy towards the hierarchy; even though the chaplains did their best to change us and to make us love the Church.'

What underlies these admissions but the expression of that spontaneous clash of working-class emotion in contact with the Church? But there is also much good will which ought to be encouraged. We must therefore help them to overcome their instinctive reactions which are so emotional and unhappy, and make them accept a faith which is more real because it is more realistic, and to learn to live in dependence, the immediate and visible fruit of which does not always seem to be apostolic fecundity.

It is then that the personal witness of the priest appears to advantage —not only his words or his help, but his life itself, in its filial, fundamental, essential attachment to our holy Mother the Church. Better than anyone else, he has the grace of his state to sustain people in this difficulty, and to lead them through it to the threshold of the Mystery. And many of our young people are capable of honestly making this transition.

(b) Another stumbling-block—apostolic responsibilities give young people a certain self-confidence and assurance which goes with the development of initiative, the habit of reflection, of questioning, and having an alert mind. Hence the restrictions of religious obedience may arouse aversion and even repugnance.

'The difficulties I am going to speak of did not, of course, spring from Catholic Action alone; one cannot be uninfluenced by the character of one's environment or of the present age or of one's former education, and, of course, there is one's own individuality.

At the very outset I can say that my somewhat dictatorial character was not set right as a result of my successive responsibilities, particularly in the Équipe Nationale. . . . My time in this Équipe also developed the spirit of independence in me, not always in the direction of true liberty. This created difficulties about authority for me at first. But now I think that under the pretext of liberty, of liberation, we chain ourselves down in independence. You know, of course, that it is not always our fault.'

We can see here again what supernatural clear-sightedness is necessary in the chaplain, to discern the element of personal satisfaction in the most generous self-giving, to lead them to welcome those redeeming trials which go with all apostolic life, to make them grow in true humility, which is the indispensable condition for entering into the mystery of God. 'I confess to thee, Father, because thou hast revealed these things to little ones.'

(c) There is a third difficulty which should be pointed out, since it constitutes a very definite and valuable field for the priest's activity:

'The discovery that Christianity embraces the whole of life, that God enters into the most ordinary every-day activities, creates in girls who have an active rather than contemplative temperament a lack of interest in, and a distaste for, the traditional religious exercises. The difficulty is increased when one's former education has laid too much stress exclusively on these exercises; or when activity, originally willed apostolically and for God, through excess or nervous lack of balance, turns into activism.

The chaplain of any girls' organisation ought to pay great attention to the extreme positions to which sudden revelations (or indeed, simple generosity) tend to drive young people. In such cases, the priest is providentially placed, both at retreats and days of recollection, as well as during the reviewing of the group's way of life, for emphasising the necessary connection between silence, prayer, regularity in approaching the sacraments, and the impregnation of activity with a living and attentive faith. It is indeed interesting to learn how frequent contemplative vocations are in both town and rural areas when there has been no preparation for this in their upbringing or early apostolic activities; it is the movement itself which made them realise both the supernatural power of prayer and the need for a total consecration of the whole of life to the glory of God, and for the benefit of all those who work or worry.

May I add that those religious houses which receive our young people from specialised movements do very much for them when their reception is materially and morally sympathetic, but they give them much more when they are able to place them in a setting of beauty and of simple and true prayer. The chaplain who has the good fortune to be able to prescribe subjects for mediattion in a community of this kind, can then put the accent on those supernatural values which are less familiar to the militants.'

(d) We can add one other difficulty.

'I had been told so often that we must be part of our milieu, that we must be like others, live like others, if we were to bring them to Christ, that I wondered how the Lord could possibly ask me to cut myself off so completely from others in the religious life . . . this was a great stumbling-block to my vocation.'

Here especially it will be the priest's task to make plain the absolute character of God's will, and to help the members live by a real faith. The perpetual search for the divine will is the antidote of this instinctive recoiling.

Another religious shows how cogent this is:

'I began by discovering the grandeur of marriage, family and social life, and their spiritual values. This may sometimes be a temptation to cast discredit on the religious life. On the other hand, it helped me to realise the meaning of it. I said to myself: If God is God, he can ask anything, even the sacrifice of these treasures.'

So at the conclusion of the first part of our report, it seems possible to affirm that specialised movements of Catholic Action, by their apostolic work which is entirely centred on the advancement of the Kingdom of God, offer a particularly favourable field for the growth of religious vocations, because they enable the Lord's appeal to be heard. But we must stress with equal force that the response of young people, the development of the germs of vocation, is largely conditional on the continuity and supernatural quality of the priest's effect on the ordinary life of the movement. Our responsibility is therefore clearly defined, and we should like to say, that, given the present outlook of young girls, specialised Catholic Action makes it easy for the priest to remain faithful to a fundamental aspect of his mission: doctrinal teaching.

What, in fact, does the experience of directors of organisations in a diocese such as Paris show? After girls reach the age of ten, there is undeniably a very considerable fall in membership in parochial groups. The causes of this are manifold, and spring from family or social developments which we are not concerned with here. Be this as it may, this numerical decline is accompanied by a poverty of religious knowledge in many adolescents and older people, even in the best Christian families. They continue to attend Sunday Mass but the nourishment their faith receives from this is too light, and is not adapted to their condition, at the very time when their intellectual powers are being developed. A school run by religious will compensate for this, provided that the young people are not unco-operative when faced with instruction which they scarcely distinguish from other subjects in the syllabus.

On the other hand, Catholic Action movements, which are unfortunately far from playing their full part, impress on us the appetite for doctrine which young people possess. Their apostolic awareness, their desire to be witnesses for Christ to their companions, awaken them to the need for a deeper understanding of religious principles. Let chaplains consider the conditions of life in which the militants live, let them grasp clearly the most serious deficiencies they have to encounter there, and, treating the obstacles as stepping-stones provided by their environment, they will have no difficulty in furnishing these young Christians with a coherent doctrinal teaching they will readily accept.

Note that we said chaplains; it is rarely one priest who undertakes the whole of the instruction. But when a young girl shares in the life of her group, at meetings, days of recollection, local or national retreats, with good will and generosity, she will slowly benefit, over the years, from a vital and progressive assimilation of the most authentic riches of the Christian revelation. Moreover, the repercussions caused by the almost inevitable failures will be only relative, for she will have acquired the habit of looking beyond these.

We are of the opinion that this doctrinal education counts for a great deal as a preparation for vocation, particularly in working class circles. Without it, young working girls will remain sentimental, and therefore superficial, Christians; and this will render the growth of the idea of vocation more difficult, and its fulfilment still more laborious, particularly as such a use of one's life can appear very unusual to working class minds, marked as they are with so many prejudices and misunderstandings.

Can we then conclude that everything necessary has been done in the Action movements? Indeed it has not; but it could be done, and the possibility is infinitely precious.

II THE ROLE OF THE PRIEST

We now come to the second part of our report—an examination of the direct part of the priest in the awakening and realisation of religious vocations in the field of specialised Catholic Action. It is clear that the chaplain's responsibilities are not at an end when he has succeeded in creating, within the movement itself, an apostolic and spiritual climate favourable to the call to complete self-oblation, so we have to ask ourselves how the chaplain to a specialised branch of Catholic Action regards religious vocation, and how he can give positive support to it. It is a complex question. The ideal chaplain does not exist, and the different reactions of individual chaplains makes it difficult to discover a common mind among them. At any rate, we can maintain that the time is past when the majority of priests evinced a certain instinctive mistrust and even hostility towards women's vocations. The confidences of many religious are eloquent of this one-time attitude of the clergy, from 'I don't believe in vocations', which one chaplain was heard to say, to 'Your duty is to look after your brothers'. This is not so say that we do not still meet this particular mentality far too frequently. Several weeks ago a superior was told by a young girl who had disclosed to a priest her conviction that she had received a call that he replied: 'A religious vocation—I don't understand what that is. Go and talk to a diocesan missionary'. But, generally speaking, we can admit that there has been some progress, some reappraisal.

So, then, the first positive aspect which we have to put forward is the importance which young people who are trying to find their way attach to the understanding approval of the priest. If, when the subject is first broached, the chaplain shows that he thinks highly of religious vocation, its value, its irreplaceable character, its mission in the Church and the world, then their search has started well.

'To know that a priest believes in our vocation,' wrote one member 'is a real strength'.

Another, who has actually entered the religious life, examines more fully the support which she received from the priesthood:

'In the movement I had to work in close co-operation with chaplains who may or may not have known of my desire to become a religious, but who had to help young people with different vocations. I can say that in them all I found the same respect and encouragement for religious vocations. I must add that if they had tried to influence me in any way, without my asking them, I should have shut up like a clam, whereas this respect expressed in prudent help was in fact the finest encouragement I could have had. With them, I discovered the grandeur of personal vocation, and the particular response which each one must give.

The two chaplains with whom I worked most always held up the religious life as something more important than a position in Catholic Action, and maintained that entry into religion ought not to be delayed in order to retain some office in a young people's organisation, still less to take on new responsibilities, save in exceptional circumstances which did not apply to me. This helped me particularly in my last year in J.A.C.F., when the call of God became more clear, and when I was being asked to remain in the movement a little longer. The only criticism I heard from a priest came from a convent chaplain, because I was not joining the Order which he served, and also because, having been helped by nursing sisters, I was going into a contemplative congregation. I was so surprised with these remarks coming from a chaplain that I was quite shaken by them.'

Beneath the sting of these remarks, there is an important message for our priestly lives, which the statement brings out clearly—we need to respect every vocation with a holy respect because all vocation comes from God, and because consecration is so absolute it has a special witness to give to the world.

'I argued that if God is God, he can ask everything, even the sacrifice of these treasures. I realised what consecration was—a witness to his transcendence, to his sovereignty over creatures.'

2. The role of the priest is not restricted to the prudent and attentive recognition of the possibility of vocation, or to its grandeur, or to a profound respect for it. It consists also in helping it, in giving positive support to it, first of all by the proper quality of his priesthood. In the many contacts with priests made in the course of Catholic Action work, the invaluable assistance afforded by the authenticity of the priest's reactions is frequently a principal factor.

'The priests who were the most help in deepening my understanding of the religious life were the curés in the villages I had occasion to pass through; the evidence of their lives of poverty and renunciation, their concern for spiritual needs, their humility in the search for ways and means, these revealed more than all the activities and discussions, the summit of the Christian life.'

Or again:

'My duties in connection with J.I.C.F. brought me into frequent contact with numerous chaplains from whom, bit by bit, I came to understand the mind of the Chruch, by listening to their arguments, seeing their reactions, and working with them. After that, as I was working in a hospital, I collaborated with the chaplain in fostering the spirit of charity there.

Every three weeks at least, I saw my spiritual father. He persuaded me to write down my examination of life each day in my militant's card . . .

Providence brought me into contact with very many chaplains, and I can say that their influence was impartial because they mutually balanced and corrected each other, and the Church's message came to me free from any excessively human element.'

Undoubtedly, this is one of the undeniable blessings of Catholic Action. It establishes a collaboration between priests and laity, which is concerned only with building the Kingdom and effecting salvation: 'I learned to understand the priest better as a result of my contacts with the chaplain; contacts which are not those of spiritual direction, but of common work.'

And the result of these many occasions of collaboration, which spring to mind at once, is that each militant is helped by the priesthood as such, rather than by Abbé X or Fr Y.

Let us add that this priestly witness attains its greatest effectiveness when prayer is obviously at the heart of the priest's ministry, as the hub of the consecrated life. The way in which they are made to pray, the tone of retreats and days of recollection, enable the call of God to sink deeply into the soul: 'After a Jiciste day of recollection, I capitulated.'

3. Finally, we come to the direct support which the chaplain of a specialised Catholic Action group can give when he is fulfilling his task as spiritual father to a militant. There are some aspects of Catholic Action which it would seem particularly advisable to emphasise.

First, the atmosphere of apostolic responsibility familiar, thanks to the movement, both to the priest and the militant. The call to total self-giving is expressed now in an extension of the activity hitherto practised, in a new form of participation in the work of Christ our Saviour, yet without any break with that which has already been performed. The one illumines the other. The deficiencies which have been noted, as well as the efforts obtained from the militants, can be examined in the light of the future demands of the religious life; thus the preparation which is always necessary before entry into religion has the great advantage of being carried out in the concrete circumstances of a life already given to the Lord, already surrendered to the dominion of charity.

The examination of life, which is the cornerstone on which the methods of Catholic Action rest, acquires a deeper significance. The search for God, and for the call of God in people and events, in effect finds itself intensified by the seal of absolute self-oblation to the Lord. The God to whom one intends to consecrate oneself entirely looks for an immediate and practical dependence in the little things which make up daily life and activity. The priest will certainly be able to teach a young girl to obey what is clearly God's will for her, because her whole formation will have rendered her attentive to the Spirit of God at work in the world.

The sacramental life itself, especially the sacrament of penance, will provide an opportunity for the chaplain to promote a right understanding of religious consecration. He will help his penitent to realise that her sin is faithlessness to the exclusive love which the Lord expects of her, and an impediment, a handicap, to the radiation of the prayer of Christ the Head, who wills through each cell of his Body to set forward his work of gathering together and salvation among men. The whole sacramental system will then be seen for what it really is— the presence and activity of Christ the Saviour among the men of our time.

Other aspects undoubtedly deserve mention. But enough has been said to show how privileged a position the priest is in for fulfilling his mission of awakening and sustaining religious vocation when this develops within the framework of some specialised group of Catholic Action, and also to remind us forcibly of our responsibilities as chaplains. We should often ask ourselves how we are carrying them out.

Having examined our own case honestly may we now ask our fellow-priests who are not Catholic Action chaplains to examine their attitude to those militants who are wondering whether they have a religious vocation? It is not uncommon in fact for such priests to watch over, help or direct young people from Catholic Action without being connected in any other way with the apostolate of the laity. And we think this is a normal state of affairs. But it could be harmful if the priest did not take into careful consideration the apostolic context in which a particular vocation was born, or at any rate grew up. Respect for the call of God involves an attentiveness to the providential conditioning which prepared and made possible the human response. Life in a Catholic Action movement, and especially the responsibilities which are undertaken to evangelise one's milieu, are major factors, essential components, governing the way in which a religious vocation develops.

This by no means implies that in choosing a particular form of the religious life the candidate must necessarily follow the line she was engaged in, in Catholic Action. The ways of God are infinite. We only hope that priests, in helping candidates, will ignore none of those elements of spiritual experience which they have acquired, and which seem to us to be of unquestioned value. This final statement from a religious will remind us not to meddle with the rather bewildering evolution of a vocation; hence the respectful prudence which every priest must show:

'In an indirect, but nevertheless very real, fashion, J.A.C.F. made me turn towards an enclosed form of the religious life, with no organised apostolate at all, however strange this may seem. It was normal to transfer on to the spiritual plane the rejection of social paternalism. Thinking that I had quite as much to receive from others as to give to them, I looked for a very simple life without any pretention as to its form, other than sharing the common lot of poverty, work and fraternity.'

This is the last of our observations. They reflect an experience which is incomplete. They emphasise the dangers to be encountered, as well as the paths to be explored. Yet their dominating theme is one of ready optimism and confidence in the possibilities of specialised Catholic Action in respect of religious vocations. This optimism, discounting the authors' legitimate affection for their work is grounded on two sets of facts:

1. The experience of the last few years shows that former militants of Catholic Action undeniably encounter difficulties during their novitiate, particularly in the sphere of obedience, and in adapting themselves to the methods of training. But once this initial purification has been successfully borne, the advantage of their experience as lay apostles is evident in the consecrated life itself.

Without being too paradoxical, we could put forward the following proposition: Novice mistresses have their work cut out with candidates from Catholic Action, but they make very fine subjects in the religious life, useful to their congregation and therefore to the Kingdom of God.

2. The second fact on which we base our confidence is the increasing number of women's vocations from Catholic Action movements at the present time, and the resultant growing co-operation between priests, religious and laity. The fact that the call to total self-oblation receives such a magnificent response from militants constitutes a seal of supernatural authenticity on the apostolic work of Catholic Action. The fact that at the same time it stimulates united effort on the part of all those responsible for these vocations, would seem to be the happy sign that they are working together as a Church. Our role as priests in all this is plain, and deserves to be fulfilled with the maximum of care and attention, because, as we hope we have shown, it is a supremely valuable factor in awakening and sustaining religious vocations.

If we may be allowed to express a hope as the final point of this report, it is that priests in every sphere may bring more and more to this very important question of religious vocation a will to mutual support and common purpose. The unanimity of priests, in this field as in many other aspects of the apostolate, constitutes one of the major factors in the edification of the Church. For our own part we, as chaplains of specialised Catholic Action, hope for this, and pray that the Lord will help us to work actively for his greater glory and the advancement of the Kingdom.

CANON FROSSARD   ABBÉ LEBRETON
Chaplain to A.C.O.   Chaplain to A.C.I.
in the Diocese of Paris.

CHAPTER XI

THE PRIEST, VOCATIONS, AND THE SCOUT MOVEMENT

BEFORE GETTING down to my own subject, I think it would be an advantage if I gave some figures showing what an important part Guiding and Scouting have played and continue to play in the recruitment of religious orders and congregations.

There are in fact, today, large numbers of former guides, guide captains and cub mistresses in our religious houses.

After reading some figures to you, I shall try to show the causes of this phenomenon by an examination of the statements I have received.

Here, then, are the findings of an inquiry conducted over several months by Fr Perrot, chaplain-general of the French Guides, who has asked me to pass them on to you. Its purpose was to ascertain the number of religious vocations among former guides.

I must repeat former guides, for similar statistics have not been obtained for former cub mistresses, since these latter do not belong to the Association of French Guides, but to its masculine counterpart, the French Scouts. We realise, of course, that some of these guides were also cub mistresses.

'We sent out a form of inquiry to every congregation and to all convents listed in the 1955 Directory—1,210 of them. We sent blue forms to those congregations which appeared to have a central novitiate, so that we could ascertain the total number of *novices* then in the novitiate. We sent yellow forms to those houses with their own novitiates, where novices remain in the same house after profession, so that we could ascertain the actual number of *nuns* in the house.

The inquiry was not appreciated everywhere. Out of the eleven hundred and twenty forms sent out, five hundred and seventy were returned, rather more than half. Some orders in which there are certainly numerous former guides did not reply. Consequently, our statistics are not complete, but the figures are none the less interesting.

168 congregations (blue forms) have no guides among their novices.

126 houses have no former guides among their professed.

The 815 religious or novices counted are distributed among:

133 congregations

143 houses.

This distribution is, actually, very uneven. In some houses, guides are extremely numerous:

The Benedictines of Vanves	21
The Trappistines of Igny	20
The Carmel at Avranches	6

Similarly, guides are numerous in some novitiates:

The Trinitarians of Valmer	6 out of 24
Canonesses Regular of St Augustine	7
Little Sisters of the Assumption	17
Sisters of St Joseph of Cluny	9

whereas other houses or novitiates possess only one or two former guides.

These figures, even though incomplete, indicate that the number of religious vocations among guides is continually growing. The findings are particularly interesting for the last few years, for which we have combined the numbers of novices returned on both types of form. Former guides who have entered religion:

1953	—	65
1954	—	95
1955	—	107
1956	—	44

Many entering in 1956 probably did so in October, are not included in the last figure.

A comparison between the number of novices included on blue forms with those on the yellow forms shows that active vocations are more numerous than contemplative, by about four to one.

Among the actives orders, vocations to the teaching orders do not appear to be very numerous.

Of the 815 enumerated, 180 had been brownies or guides only, all the rest had been rangers or guide captains; 181 had only been guides for two years or less. The rest had been guides for three years at least. This seems to indicate that guiding left its mark on them and brought them to the threshold of the religious life.'

Although we ourselves have not conducted a similar inquiry to ascertain the number of former cub mistresses now in religion, we did send a questionnaire to a large number of them, the answers to which form the basis for the report which follows.

I had better give you the substance of this questionnaire, although it goes beyond the strict scope of this report, which is limited to the role of the priest; you will then be in a position to see from what context I have drawn the information.

1. Did you already know of your religious vocation before you became a guide or cub mistress?

2. Do you consider that you owe your religious vocation to your experience in the Scout movement?

3. If you had a vocation before joining, did your membership of the movement strengthen it? Or make it more clear?

4. Did your experience of the movement have anything to do with your choice of Order or Congregation? (choice of an active rather than a contemplative order, or vice versa).

5. Can you say which values discovered in the movement might have led you to think of the religious life? Can you remember anything that might have been decisive in your progress towards it?

6. Did the chaplain's presence, and your collaboration with him, help you to contemplate the religious life? to dispose you towards it?

7. Did your membership of the scout movement help you to discover the value of the religious life? to dispel any prejudices you entertained towards the religious life in general, and certain orders in particular?

You will see that we are here concerned only with the replies to Question 6. Since these were in general extremely interesting, I thought it right quite simply to pass on to you their substance.

Out of around two hundred questionnaires sent out, I received nearly one hundred and thirty replies.

I grouped the replies under headings, which came into my mind as I went through the files and I propose to give you the most telling replies and comment where necessary.

In conclusion I shall put forward a few thoughts arising from these statements which, I hope, will throw some light on the role of the scout chaplain in awakening vocations within the movement.

By this method my report describes what in fact the role of the priest *is or has been*, according to the statements of the religious, rather than what it *ought to be*; but it seems to me that a priest can learn what he must do to be a good instrument in awakening vocations just as well from the results of practical experience as from the abstract principles and directions.

I have already observed that the influence of the scout chaplain in awakening vocations is frequently indirect. Some point out that their chaplain helped them to discover not the religious life as such, but just the Christian life.

A Little Sister of P. de Foucauld writes:

'The presence of a chaplain helped me to envisage, not the religious life as such, but the Christian life.'

A Poor Clare:

'A first retreat for cub mistresses, preached by Fr X made me conscious of my Christianity and of the necessity of a profound interior life.'

An enclosed Dominican:

'Working with my pack and district chaplains contributed largely to putting me on to the religious life, although I never discussed the matter with them.'

Many make a point of saying that the priest's presence was an influence but not a determining one in the decision to enter religion, or in the choice of a congregation.

An Augustinian Canoness:

'Our chaplain was a young, reserved, but very apostolic curate from the cathedral, and he gave proof of unusual vigour in his ministry, as he suffered from a serious illness. He did not husband his strength—I saw this for myself at our summer camp, and I saw his asceticism too. He had to drive many miles each morning to say Mass for us. I was impressed by his gentle kindness, but in no other way did he influence my vocation.'

A Poor Clare:

'Personally, I think the chaplain's presence and co-operation were indirectly a help in making me think about the religious life. He gave a good deal of time to our instruction, laying great stress upon this particular aspect of his ministry, and he made us deepen our knowledge of the scout law so that we could live it to the full.'

A Sister of the Sacred Heart:

'His willing attention to the needs of every one, his instructions, which were always so profound, the atmosphere of respect and simplicity created around him, and especially the liturgical formation which he sought to give us, all contributed to that enrichment which I owe to my years as cub mistress.'

A Dominican:

'An indirect influence was perhaps those farewell parties we had for guides entering the convent.'

A Benedictine:

'The chaplains apparently helped me much more by their presence—i.e. God with us—than by their words.'

A Cistercian:

'One of the Fathers was very concerned with everything connected with the pack and the meetings of cub mistresses even if he were away; without him it would not have been Scouting. His presence, to say nothing of his moral help and his encouragement, helped me to believe in the movement.'

A Visitation nun:

'The chaplain's part in my vocation was a very discreet one. It was a long time before I told him about it—I thought that he was observing my life and probably guessed many things. But whenever I needed clear and positive direction I approached him confidently, sure that he would interpret the will of the Lord for me. I only wanted one word from him, the decisive word which would confirm or interpret my inner light, and I had this word every time I needed it.'

This last statement indicates a more direct and decisive influence on the part of the scout chaplain, and it occurs in other replies as well. But before passing on to this, I should like to emphasise the great importance of the indirect influence of a priest whose life is observed at close quarters, the evidence of whose example makes an impression and begets the desire for a life consecrated to the Lord.

Indeed, some of the replies are quite explicit about the part played by the chaplain's example.

A Little Sister of P. de Foucauld:

'Our chaplain was a very earnest man, and inculcated the meaning and importance of fraternal charity into us older guides. It was this that led me to the service of the sick, and later to our form of contemplative and missionary life. Yes, to see the way a religious lived was a great lesson to me.'

We will now quote some of the statements which show a more direct and decisive influence.

A Little Sister of P. de Foucauld:

'During a retreat preached by Fr X to the cub mistresses, I was hesitating between two ways. Father said: "Try; that is what novitiates are for". At another retreat I made the acquaintance of a scout chaplain who then became my director and confirmed my aspirations: "I think you were made for the total oblation".'

A Daughter of St Martha:

'A chaplain at the height of his priestly life; working with him: for me, these things were decisive in turning my thoughts towards the religious life.'

A Dominican of Bethany:

'During a meeting for the young girls of the parish, the question of religious vocation came up, and, to my own great surprise, I found myself refuting all those objections put forward by one or other of the girls, which hitherto I myself had held. I confided in the Father, an Assumptionist, and told him of this self-contradiction, and, on his advice, made a five day retreat, during which I said "Yes" to God. The retreat ended, and I knew that I must be a religious.'

A Little Sister of the Assumption:

'I should like to mention the part played by the chaplain, a Jesuit Father, who in a most self-effacing, and perhaps therefore more profound, way, preached a three day recollection as part of our course. What impressed me was the insistence with which he spoke to me about the marks of detachment and ransom which already foreshadowed the character of my religious life. I think three out of the eleven rangers present decided during this course to enter religion. The following Pentecost the same Jesuit Father preached a recollection day and brought up the problem of factory-girls; this recollection day was instrumental in directing my vocation towards the workers, and in my choice of the congregation of the Little Sisters of the Assumption.'

A Benedictine:

'After twenty-five years in a contemplative community, I am still marked by the influence of my first chaplains, with whom I worked so closely.'

A Dominican:

'I had as my director the district chaplain, who was a great help in disposing me, through the Scout movement, for the religious life. The war came, and separated me from him. I had dealings with many pack chaplains. My work with one of them brought enrichment in my training as a cub mistress, and indirectly for the religious life. I think this influence varies a great deal with the personality of the chaplains and the extent to which they possess the scout spirit. They can be a great help in the life of the district and in the summer schools. If I sought out the chaplain of Chamarande, it was because of his extraordinary influence. He was very demanding about our scout life, which he shared with enthusiasm, yet he wove the supernatural into it quite naturally. I subsequently worked as a cub mistress with him, and he was my director until he was deported. He helped a great deal in making my scouting an immediate preparation for the religious life, yet he did not hesitate to make me restrict my scouting activities because they were interfering with my studies.'

A Poor Clare:

'It was during a recollection day for cub mistresses that I met the chaplain, a Franciscan Father, who was able to discern better than I could that divine call which had been buried for ten years. He was indeed the Lord's instrument for rescuing me (for I was going through a difficult period) and for taking me to himself, in spite of initial resistance. He was a tower of strength to me during the inevitable conflicts, and always looked after me.'

A Poor Clare:

'It was at a social evening for cub mistresses that the question of religious vocation was broached by our chaplain for the first time. He spoke about it with conviction, inviting us to consider this matter fairly, as an eventuality which was just as possible and desirable as marriage. He declared that in principle there ought to be a religious vocation in one person out of three, and that if it does not work out like this in practice it is largely because of lack of generosity. This interlude impressed us all very much, without giving us the slightest desire to enter religion. But the seed had certainly been sown, and could not fail to germinate if God gave it an opportunity. As far as I was concerned, this happened two months later during a group Mass. As I was receiving Holy Communion I clearly heard the Lord's call: "Do you not wish to be my religious, too?" My first reaction was: "What a blow. I don't want to enter the convent at all." But I was ready to do God's will. I waited only for clearer light. I approached my director again about it, and he urged me to pray.'

A Visitation nun:

'It seems right to emphasise the importance of the presence and co-operation of the chaplain. In my own case, the priest—he really was a priest—was the channel of the decisive light, the tracking-sign leading me to my encounter with the Lord.'

A religious of Our Lady of Chevilly:

'The chaplain added the finishing touches, and gave me a good shaking up. After that, I made my decision!'

A Little Sister of the Assumption:

'It was the pack chaplain who helped me to realise that I had a vocation. He was so sincere, and made no attempt to make things seem easy. Rather the contrary, but with much tact and firmness, and gaiety too, he helped me to get out of myself and to find joy.'

On reading their statements we shall see that for some of them it was the fact that they were cub mistresses that led them to discover what the priest and priesthood are. For hitherto they had known the priest only as a distant personage cloistered in the sanctuary of the church for the ceremonies, in the confessional for imposing a penance, and in the presbytry for administering the parish.

A Little Sister of the Assumption:

'Working with a chaplain led me to discover something which I had never realised before: the priest's activity outside church.'

For many, being cub mistresses led them to discover that they needed a spiritual director. And the chaplain, having become their director, drew them on to the religious life.

A Daughter of Charity:

'We often used to talk with our group chaplain about the religious life as well as marriage, and he dwelt at great length on our future lives, on the preparation and prayer necessary for the days to come. He was my first director of conscience, since I had not felt the need for one before, and did not see what purpose he could serve.'

A Carmelite:

'To be more personal, it was to a chaplain that I first mentioned my longing for the religious life, and it was our company chaplain who became my spiritual director.'

A Sister of the Presentation:

'I hardly profited by all the chaplain could have done for me, since I did not acquaint him with my ambition for the religious life until a few months before I left for the novitiate; but after that he did not miss a single opportunity of preparing me for the total oblation, letting me see all the sacrifices which my too independent nature, my too self-sufficient character, would be required to make; kindly and patiently correcting the false ideas which I had fabricated for myself.'

A Canoness of St Augustine:

'I received much good advice from the chaplain I had taken for my director. He certainly helped me very much to realise my vocation.'

I should like to observe now that it is not only the particular group chaplain with whom the cub mistress habitually works, who plays a part in the awakening of her vocation, but often also the occasional priest she may meet in the course of a social evening, a recollection day or a retreat.

A missionary Sister:

'I did not actually work with the chaplain who helped and advised me, since he was not our group chaplain. But I have never lost touch with him. He is now old, sick and retired, yet his letters are still full of fire and spirit and a wonderful understanding.'

An enclosed Dominican:

'The Dominican Father who had advised me to take up scouting preached the annual retreat for cub mistresses two years in succession, and this certainly turned my thoughts towards a Dominican congregation. Dominican spirituality was an admirable perpetuation and completion of the discoveries begun in scouting. In my case the chaplain, as chaplain, played no part.'

This leads me to say a few words about the importance for the awakening of vocations of the numerous retreats, recollection days, pious outings and pilgrimages which take place in the movement, and in which the priest plays a leading part.

A Franciscan Missionary of Mary:

'Each year we made a three day retreat with all the cub mistresses from the Versailles and Saint-Cloud districts. These retreats had a profound influence on my spiritual life. It was as a result of one of them that I decided to take a spiritual father, who was none other than our district chaplain himself. Without him, it is unlikely that my vocation would have come to anything.'

A Benedictine:

'It was indeed during a cub camp that, influenced by the chaplain, a former cub master, I began to think of the religious life. He then began to direct me. Some months later I made a retreat with the district cub mistresses, where I discovered the primordial value of prayer, silence, penitence and humility (strict silence reigned until the end of the retreat). I decided to enter the Order.'

A Benedictine:

'I did not give a thought to the religious life until I made a retreat with my troop at the abbey where I was later to make my profession. A retreat in which, in silence and real prayer, I prepared to take the ranger promise. This was followed up by a pious outing and by a camp which was richly blessed. From this, I awoke quite gently to my vocation.'

A Daughter of Charity:

'The annual cub mistresses' retreat was our principal opportunity for reflection. It was actually at one of these that I met a priest, a scout chaplain, who, without any pressure, helped to put me on the way to the religious life which I had glimpsed, and to appreciate its value more deeply. Hence the fundamental role of a holy and supernatural priest, having no preconceived ideas himself, but simply helping the soul to find its way.'

A White Sister:

'I can tell you quite simply that the idea of vocation came to me immediately after a retreat for cub mistresses, preached by a Father who never mentioned the subject at all.'

An Ursuline:

'Scouting was also a great support for my spiritual life through the chaplain's explanations and the discussions we had with him at our meetings, in camp, at recollection days, at retreats, through articles in reviews, the work done in preparation for cub-meetings, and also through the times of prayer we shared together.'

A Benedictine:

'The visits we made in several years during Holy Week to Benedictine houses were also occasions of joy and spiritual plenitude which I shall never forget. I remember that I left this monastic life with an acute nostalgia and a desire, longing rather, to share it. It is certain that these contacts with the Church's liturgical life and with her prayer of praise helped to bring to light the deep aspirations within me. I think it was after the last visit, to La Pierre-qui-Vire, that I began to read the Layfolk's Breviary.'

I now come to the combined influence of the chaplain and the specific framework of scout life—camp, the open air, nature. The dangers of Naturism and Pantheism which beset a religious soul immersed in Scouting have been pointed out often enough. But if the priest is wise he will know how to avoid, and to help others to avoid, these dangers, and camp life can be a wonderful opportunity and environment for fostering certain vocations.

A Dame of the Holy Cross of Jerusalem:

'The chaplain's presence and my work with him directed my thoughts towards the religious life, and it was notably a word spoken by him at the end of a camp fire that had the greatest influence on my vocation.'

A Cistercian:

'I found a great deal of tact and understanding in our pack chaplain. He always threw himself enthusiastically into the programmes and the meetings, despite the heavy responsibilities of his ministry. I think this was a fundamental factor. The spiritual authority must be above agitations and material preoccupations if he is to train leaders to be silent and recollected, to reflect and to listen, so that they may obtain that light and strength which are then multiplied a hundredfold because drawn from God. It is this foundation of the interior life that must be emphasised, and I find that nothing is better able to move scouts in this direction than well-conducted meditations by the camp chaplain. Meditations made in the open air at dawn, when all nature is awakening. The soul unites with nature to praise the Lord. In the silence of the noon-day, and in the evening after camp-fire when silence descends once again, make a silent watch in union with the silence of nature, in which one finds the Great and Living God who lives in very silence. It was beneath the great oaks and in the woods that our Father St Bernard learnt, as he tells us, more than from books. We have in Scouting an instrument of the finest quality for helping souls to awaken to their vocation! It was in the silences of the camp that my own soul was forged. The soul learns to listen, to reflect, to decide.'

If we ask ourselves now, rather more precisely, where the real influence of the scout chaplain in the awakening of vocations lies, we shall find—apart from the personal contacts of spiritual direction—that it is exerted especially in three spheres:

1. In the liturgical life which is lived at training camps or summer schools intensively but with complete sincerity.

2. In the doctrinal teaching which is given by the chaplain at the summer schools or at instruction classes throughout the year.

3. In co-operation in apostolic work every day throughout the year.

1. LITURGICAL LIFE IN CAMP

Many emphasise first the part the chaplain played in the camp-schools where they went to learn their job as cub mistresses.

A Dominican:

'I was studying to be a social worker. At the same time I felt the need to discover what my future congregation was to be. It was after I had made various investigations in vain that I went to Chamarande, very anxious because I had found nothing corresponding to what I was looking for—and I told the chaplain of my difficulty. He named the community at once; it had been founded several years ago, and he knew of it through a guide captain. I found everything I had hoped for there, and much more.'

A Carmelite:

'I should like to stress the influence of camp-schools, especially C.N.E., where we really discovered and deepened our Christian life. Active participation in the Mass led me to a better understanding of its meaning, and the lectures inspired us to a more active search for God.'

2. DOCTRINAL TEACHING

A Third Order Dominican

'The chaplain's doctrinal teaching compelled me not to be satisfied with a facile piety and little stories in my talks to the guides, but to live the doctrine, and to obtain a deeper knowledge of it, so that I could prepare them better for the Father's teaching.'

A Benedictine:

'The chaplain's influence was not direct, but his explanations of the Gospel were a help.'

An enclosed Dominican:

'I must emphasise the fact that it was the doctrinal riches of the Order, patiently passed on by the chaplain, that dispelled all my objections (it is perhaps not unimportant to point this out to a congress of priests), and also the sight of a wonderful religious life completely aware of all the problems of the present day.'

A Sister of the Sacred Heart:

'For myself, I am almost certain that, although I was not actually aware of it at the time, guiding contributed largely to my rediscovery of the vocation which had been stifled in my early years. Later, when I became a cub mistress, a single fact was responsible for moving me—a week-end pilgrimage, the theme of which was "Vocation, the Call". This week-end was attended by local cub masters and mistresses. I remember very distinctly the talk on "The Call, from Abraham to ourselves" and "How the called responded". It is the only occasion of which I can really say that I was aware of being drawn to the religious life.'

A Marist sister:

'The chaplain's presence at pack meetings or meetings of cub mistresses helped me to expand, and I got used to talking to priests, a thing I had never dared to do before, though such timidity is certainly rather silly. These contacts gave me confidence in the priest, and when I had difficulties to overcome I did not hesitate to tell my chaplain about them, and was happy to accept his advice. It was certainly he who helped me over the last stile and prepared me to enter the novitiate. I also owe a great deal to the district chaplain, who, through his study circles, helped me to acquire a firmer grasp of my religion.'

A Little Sister of the Assumption:

'It is the principal role of our chaplains, who take part in our activities with such unsparing zeal, to lead us to a personal consideration of the demands of our service, to make us do some deep doctrinal thinking, to stimulate fruitful exchanges of opinion (notably on the different courses open to us, the different vocations in life), and to help us to harmonise principles with living.'

A White Sister:

'By his meditations, his short commentaries at Mass, and his recollection days, our first district chaplain brought us right to the very heart of the Church. I can still remember some of his vivid expressions, which were really enlightening. The second chaplain, who knew me better, and who accompanied us on several cub camps and leaders' outings, inspired us with the spirit of Carmel: the spirit of renunciation and contemplation.'

3. THE BIRTH OF APOSTOLIC ARDOUR. It can come from close collaboration with the chaplain's apostolic activity.

From Dominican:

'I think it was contact with the chaplains more than anything else that aroused apostolic ardour in me. I worked with them at pack meetings, and also in other matters which, strictly, went beyond these limits. This contact with the problems of a parochial apostolate was probably the origin of my desire to assist the priests, and to work as one of a team with them, a desire which led me towards the Congregation of the *Dominicaines Missionaires des Campagnes*, which exists for such co-operation with the clergy. On coming into contact with them I discovered the demands of the consecrated life, which permits of no compromise, and whose only concern is for the advancement of the Kingdom of God and ... solitude. And that was no deterrent to my vocation—rather the contrary.'

A Sister of Charity:

'Actually, our pack chaplains were young priests, and this being so I would not have dreamed of seeking their support for becoming a religious. But our collaboration was effective, truly apostolic, full of fraternal help. I am sure that this co-operation with the chaplain was extremely valuable for me, particularly from the apostolic point of view. This common concern for the welfare of souls creates a team spirit with the priests which, in a way, is irreplaceable. From this point of view, scouting gave us the perfect training, and this apostolic spirit shared by leaders and chaplains, is an enrichment for both.'

I should not be presenting a true picture, I am sure, unless I gave you the negative side of the balance sheet as well. So I will now note some of the limitations of the influence exercised by the chaplains. Some statements explain these limitations by the fact that the chaplains are frequently too self-sufficient.

A Benedictine:

'Our cub chaplain was really too self-sufficient for any real co-operation with us. But his supernatural attitude was, for the mistresses as well as for the cubs, representative of the grandeur of the religious life.'

A Third Order Dominican:

'The chaplains at that time, as now, were overwhelmed by their work, and I do not think they were sufficiently free to give effective help to a cub mistress on the personal level. Often we had time only for bringing up matters connected with the pack—sixers, cubs, etc.—and these were very numerous, for we really loved our cub work. When the cub mistresses of the district met for their instructions, questions were difficult, for in my case the chaplain was the same priest as for the pack, and the time factor was terrible.'

A Little Sister of P. de Foucauld:

'Unfortunately, the only chaplains I ever had could give us only very little time, and we had not much chance of working with them; and this, it seems to me, is a matter for regret.'

A Carmelite:

'Unfortunately, the chaplain was not much help to me; I did not see very much of him, which is not unusual for a cub chaplain. They often consider the cubs uninteresting. They are too small! But this is a pity. As a result, my activities in the parish were rather thwarted! When I did see him, we talked about the cubs—but nothing personal. No help or encouragement for my vocation from that quarter.'

I will also mention some warnings and criticisms about the chaplain's attitude.

A Canoness of St Augustine:

'To be quite frank, I was often rather surprised at the familiarity of some of the cub mistresses with the chaplains, usually young curates. To my twenty years it seemed that the priest had a transcendence which should have called for more reserve on the part of the girls. My respect for the priest also told me that young curates should have been more distant.'

A Dominican:

'A religious who was a friend of the family told me that I was good only for playing at cops and robbers. This expression, so lacking in psychological insight, made a profound impression, and I jumped at the opportunity to reject the idea of the religious life. Without scouting, it is highly possible that I should have refused the call of Christ, intoxicated by my years at the Sorbonne, following this remark. There is so much facile talk about marriage, and far too little mention of the religious life.'

A Daughter of Charity:

'At every retreat I attended, when the vocation of women was mentioned it was almost invariably marriage that was envisaged. "The religious vocation is a thing apart", and so the subject was shelved. In 1954 the Easter retreat for girls in my parish was preached by a scout chaplain who admitted having swotted up the Handbook for Cub Mistresses before the retreat, though he made no allusion to scouting in his talks. He declared that "a great deal is said about marriage, but there are two other vocation for girls, about which not so much is said—celibacy, and the religious vocation; and it is about these that we shall speak"; and he emphasised vigorously the grandeur of consecrated virginity.'

A Little Sister of the Assumption:

'Despite my vocation, thus abruptly but surely discovered, I still retained numerous prejudices against the religious life, and dreamed of something which would resemble it inwardly by vows and community life, but not outwardly. Except for my Ranger Captain and a Jesuit Father, scouting was no help in dispelling these particular prejudices. Even a curate whom I had met several times (not in connection with scouting, though he was, in fact, chaplain to some guides and brownies) appeared not to favour this kind of life, though he was very discreet about it. Many priests seem to be unacquainted with the religious life; witness the case of the young curate who, when asked to preach at a renewal of promises, said: "I don't know anything that I can compare it with".'

Some lack of understanding on the part of the secular clergy:

A Dominican:

'The presence of secular priests was no help to me at all. I came across many in the course of my rounds, in common work, at retreats . . . one advised me to take up the lay apostolate, others met the announcement of my departure with a distinct silence; one said he could not understand it, because I should play a much more effective part if I remained in the world as a lay apostle. Their lack of understanding, their misunderstanding of the religious life for women, I found quite startling; contacts with religious were my only help.'

A Religious of Nevers:

'Yes, the chaplain's presence is valuable. But it is not every chaplain who understands the full worth of the religious life, and sometimes their only thought is that their pack will be without a cub mistress if she leaves for the convent. Then they try to show how valuable is a life dedicated to the aposto-late. Moreover, some priests have no liking for the religious life, and don't believe in it; they like to think of themselves as in the van of progress and fearfully up to date, so they discourage vocations, deeming them useless.'

A Sister of Jesus Réparateur:

'My membership of the movement was at first a hindrance to my vocation, since I was influenced by certain chaplains who did not approve of my giving up scouting. In the grip of my zeal for my job as captain and commissioner, I thought for a while that my scouting service would be a substitute for the religious life.'

To conclude these citations, which would otherwise become mono-tonous, here are two final statements which seem to me to be most typical in revealing the role of the priest in the awakening of vocations. Both clearly testify to a close and apostolic collaboration with the priest. The first stresses the importance of that sure and objective know-ledge of the girls which the chaplain will obtain as a result of this common apostolic work, while the second gives weight to that interior knowledge which comes from the spiritual direction occasioned by some scouting activity.

A White Sister:

'The presence of a chaplain. . . . It is a fact that the two priests who helped me to become conscious of my vocation and to follow it were two scout chaplains. It was through scout activities that I met them, but it seems that scouting only played an extraneous part in it. It was not because they were chaplains or because I was working with them that their presence helped me. But it is probable that their help was more effective because they knew me better, and from the outside, if I may say so . . . they had seen me at work, knew what the others thought about me . . . instead of just knowing me through my confidences . . . and I think that enabled them to advise me in a much more certain fashion.'

A Sister of Charity:

'It was through their agency that my vocation was suddenly revealed to me, one morning. During a camp which was morally difficult because of the easy-

going ways of the mistress, our chaplain's constant availability, his supernatural wisdom and power of appeasement were the immediate instruments
of the Lord's call. After the first enthusiasm of this thunderbolt which over-
threw all my plans, the encouragement and advice of my chaplain, whom I
trusted, and who knew me through our routine meetings and collaboration in
running a very lively and active group, were indispensable in helping me to
believe in my vocation and to fulfil it. I have often told myself that without
him during the two years which were darkness rather than light, I should
not be where I am now, and happy because I am doing what I was meant
to do.'

The fact that clearly emerges from this report is that in the Church
in France at the present time, guiding and scouting, among other
movements, provide privileged opportunities for girls to meet and
collaborate with the priest, and in consequence they are a marvellous
field for the awakening of religious vocations.

We have seen from these statements that the priest makes an impression on these girls, these vocations, first of all by his presence, before
ever he speaks or acts. We do not sufficiently appreciate the importance
of the mere contact of a generous young girl with a priest bearing an
authentically priestly witness.

These repeated contacts, prolonged during the weeks in camp, are
privileged occasions when the priest can show his priesthood in its
true light. And he can do so under exceptionally favourable conditions.
He is available, and is not concerned with the responsibilities of practical organisation; he is thus able to interest himself in the personal
problems of the guides and cub mistresses.

It is enough for him just to be a true priest among them, to know
how to listen, to have the ability to say the right word at the right time
—either to all of them, or to one in particular—about some religious
congregation, when passing near a monastery, or when somebody
enters the convent, or when a letter arrives from a religious who was
a former cub mistress, for the germ of vocation to spring up in emi-
nently favourable, prepared ground.

I am more and more convinced that to be a cub mistress these days,
and to do the job well, young girls must have such a measure of zeal,
such a feeling for others, and for the interior life, that the Holy Spirit,
who knows quite well who are the most likely instruments for his
purpose, must often prowl around this particular flock for his
prey.

'The first thing', reveals a former cub mistress, now a Little Sister of the Assumption, 'which gave me the idea of the possibility of the religious life, was my first cub camp. One evening, after an exceptionally hard day, I realised all at once that I hadn't had time to think of myself at all, and that, although very tired, I was completely happy.'

FR. HEGO, O.F.M.,
National Chaplain to the Cubs.

CHAPTER XII

THE ROLE OF THE DIOCESAN DIRECTOR OF RELIGIOUS

IT WAS VERY rash of me to agree to speak to this Congress about the role of the Diocesan Director of Religious in the awakening of vocations—partly because this work is quite new to me, and I have not been doing it for very long; I am a parish priest in the process of transformation! Partly, also, because the art of putting what I feel into words does not come easily to me, but most of all because I am in danger of repeating, and badly at that, what Canon Lieutier has written so well in recent numbers of *Vocations sacerdotales et religieuses*.

As a diocesan priest whose charge lies more particularly, if not exclusively, with religious, I feel nevertheless as though I am in the market-place. I am in touch with religious more than anyone else, but I do meet the clergy and to some extent the faithful laity.

From this vantage point it is possible to have a view of the situation as a whole. I hear the same remarks, the same aspirations, the same complaints; I see the same gaps and the same needs, and so it becomes easy and sometimes urgent to convey to those who must be informed —authority, our fellow priests, religious, the faithful themselves— the observations which have been gathered here.

'Exactly where do we stand on this question of women's religious vocations?' This, in a nutshell, is the question which was forced on my mind and inspired my inquiries, when I learnt of the withdrawal of religious from places where they had been stationed for many years, and when I found myself in the presence of parish priests, mayors, representatives of school boards, and delegates from hospital management committees, who had the increasingly difficult and even pointless task of finding a congregation to take the place of that which had given notice of its departure, and had adhered to its decision, often despite the intervention of episcopal authority.

The same question was brought to my notice still more forcibly when I heard the desperate plea of the majority of superiors general for vocations to be found and sent to them, so that they could continue to meet the requirements of those good works for which they were responsible, and not have to close any more houses or give way to the understandable temptation of allowing their subjects to remain only where they were at the present time.

An inquiry was launched covering the fifteen monasteries and thirty-one mother houses established in the diocese of Lyons. It was an incomplete inquiry, but, as far as it went, capable of furnishing a true and fair view of the situation as a whole.

To the question: 'Give the number—year by year, from 1920 to 1945—of religious professions in your congregation', the replies were rather a long time in arriving. It was actually necessary after some months to remind some of the defaulters who did not appreciate the importance of this inquiry. Moreover, the examination of a defective balance sheet is never pleasant, but it can be salutary.

The figures received show that the annual number of religious professions during the period between the wars was almost constant. But taking as a whole the period following the 1939 war they reveal a general fall in the region of some 30 per cent at least; this has been particularly noticeable during the past few years, and tends to become more pronounced.

In a diocese such as Lyons in which the very different mentalities of city- and country-dwellers meet, and areas differ widely from the point of view of religion—practising and non-practising, Christian and less Christian—we observe a drying-up of women's religious vocations almost everywhere, except—and this exception is noteworthy—where an impetus given by consecrated souls has been sustained by consecrated souls (priests and religious), illustrating the truth that example prevails, and is better than precept.

Certain rural areas seem to have felt the evil effects more than others. Before dis-establishment almost every parish in these areas had its religious community. One of the consequences of dis-establishment was the suppression of a large number of them, and even those which managed to survive are in process of gradually disappearing for want of young candidates to replace those who are getting on in years. Together with the depopulation of these areas, the departure of the sisters is one of the causes of the decrease in the number of vocations.

I gave these figures first to the diocesan authority, then to the rural deans, on the occasion of the half-yearly meeting at Easter. A negative sort of action, undoubtedly, but one which had the import and significance of an S.O.S. Revealing the extent of the decline in the number of vocations, it drew attention to the danger that threatened, in the immediate future, the apostolic expansion and even the very existence of so many good works which could continue only with difficulty without the presence of religious. It is therefore a matter of urgency that we should concern ourselves more, and very quickly, with the discerning and fostering of religious vocations.

A religious profession is a vocation which has come to fulfilment. But there are many vocations these days which do not come to fulfilment. There is wanting either the climate necessary for their growth and development or gardeners who are able and willing to tend them.

We simply cannot believe that God, who is so prodigal of the seed of life in nature, is niggardly in the field of vocations, where immortal souls are concerned. For the greater perfection of some of these souls results in the salvation of a still greater number of others.

There is a shortage of religious, but there are some young girls who are contemplating the religious life. Many of them dare not speak about it, and they have to find their way alone. Those who feel called to give themselves wholly and exclusively to God, to serve him either in prayer and penitence or in devotion to their brethren, will have to battle with their environment, often against their family, always against prejudice and certainly against themselves. Let us realise what a struggle this can be when they have to endure it for many years in a world which is hostile to their vocation.

People still accept quite readily a boy's vocation to the priesthood, but as a rule they appear reserved about, and even opposed to, a girl's vocation to the religious life. During the scholastic year 1952–3, a parish priest was very worried since he had to find a congregation which would agree to take over the secondary school of some two hundred pupils in his parish, because the religious in charge of the school had informed the Committee confidentially that they would have to leave at the beginning of October.

To find another congregation was not easy, even with the concurrence and support of the Diocesan Director of Independent Schools. Many steps had to be taken, many letters written. The pearl of great price was finally discovered only a few days before the end of May. Deo Gratias!

Now a few days after agreement had been reached with the new congregation, the parish priest happened to be talking to two members of the school Committee after their monthly meeting—a man and a woman, both of them parents of children in the school. The man said: 'Tell me, Father, why has it been so difficult to find religious to take over from those who are leaving?' The reply came readily: 'There are not enough vocations these days' . . . upon which the man, who had only two children, both girls, declared: 'If I had any boys, I should be proud if one of them became a priest; but one of my daughters a religious? No! Not that!' And before the parish priest could say a word the woman affirmed: 'I have two boys and two girls, and if one of my sons wanted to be a priest I should willingly allow him to do so, but I should not be happy if one of my daughters told me that she wanted to be a religious!' I will leave you to guess what the priest's reply was. But does not this story from real life indicate one of the causes of the lack of religious vocations?

Thus, even in practising families, who make such sacrifices for the Christian education of their children, and have such complete confidence in religious, there is so little esteem for the religious life that they are afraid of it and dread it; the religious life is not understood because it is not known; people's ideas about it are so distorted as to be completely false.

Forgive me for introducing a personal note, but the following little story does seem to me to indicate the state of mind about religious and hence the religious life, its very real difficulties as well as its beauty, its merits and its profound worth.

As a rule, when a person is appointed to a new post he receives congratulations and good wishes. When I was nominated for my present position, and it was known that I was going to work with religious and should therefore be leaving parish work—heavy though it was— almost everywhere, I was extremely attached to it—from my parishioners in every walk of life, as well as from many fellow priests, I heard hardly anything but: 'Oh, I *am* sorry for you!'—always the same, always spoken in the same tone of commiseration, and hardly encouraging. Does not this little anecdote reveal an attitude of mind? They mean it as a joke, perhaps; but fundamentally they are a little doubtful of the real value of the religious life of the sisters, whose services nevertheless they look for and appreciate. How can religious vocations spring up and flower against the background of a mental attitude such as this? We must put it right.

But I am not going to complain—I want to make this clear, after three years of this work. I meet difficulties, true enough. Who doesn't? But more important are the fine souls I meet, given entirely to God and devoted to others, despite the material destitution and spiritual isolation in which some of them find themselves.

There is a shortage of religious, but are we trying hard enough to find them?

For many years—about thirty at least, in our case—great efforts have been made, not without success, on behalf of vocations to the priesthood. But we have got to recognise that a similar effort, which ought normally to be parallel and simultaneous, has not been made for vocations to the religious life.

'We have heard a good deal about vocations to the priesthood, and rightly; but why is so little said about vocation to the religious life?' In the course of my visits to communities I have so often heard this complaint from the lips of religious, whom I felt were profoundly troubled; yet it was without any bitterness or acrimony, and even rather timidly, since they would not wish it to be taken as a criticism.

A less frequent remark, but alas how sad, is this which I have heard on several occasions: 'If I am a religious, it is no thanks to the priest at home: he did not encourage me very much'. Does this not indicate a failure to understand, a lack of interest, and perhaps even opposition?

Opposition? I wish we could doubt it. But facts are facts. I do not think I can accuse the Superior General who made the following remark of exaggerating very much.

'People only think about us when we're at death's door. We close a house. . . . What a storm of protest! But who ever thinks of keeping us alive, of sending us recruits?'

Or this one:

'If priests would only tend the seeds of vocation, there would be more of them.'

It is God who gives the vocation. It is he who calls. But as a rule the priest is the instrument of the divine choice. His agency is necessary to bring home to his people its existence and grandeur: to the children at catechism, to the young people, to adults in Catholic Action and devotional organisations, to all his parishioners through personal contact, through his parish magazine, by Vocations Days, at clothings, at golden jubilees, silver jubilees, celebrations to honour a religious who has been in the parish or doing the same work for many years. These events are evidence of sympathy and recognition, of respect and esteem.

It is the priest's duty to discern the vocation, to awaken it, to make the subject aware of it, to guide it while respecting both the activity of God and the liberty of the subject.

A fellow priest, still young, who is occupied with this serious problem of women's religious vocations, writes:

'There is a shortage of religious vocations but very few priests imagine this to be the case! Could it be that insufficient attention is paid to possible vocations?

They do not understand the psychology of girls in the matter of vocation, their various crises: how they lose the idea of entering religion at the age of adolescence, then take it up again at fifteen or twenty. They are unaware of their differing reactions: the denial and criticism of vocation which mean, as a rule, that they are thinking about it.

They are not sufficiently conscious of the factors which favour vocations: retreats, membership of some special and militant Catholic Action group, spiritual direction, and reading.

They are not aware that they must encourage them, all the more because they have to struggle for so long without any help such as is provided, for example, by seminary life.'

I understand now why Mgr Ancel invited me to speak to priests on their days of recollection when he appointed me Diocesan Director of Religious. When I asked to be excused, pleading my incompetence and my work with religious, which I could foresee would be engrossing, he replied: 'Yes. You will keep in touch with the priests, and talk to them about the sisters.'

I regarded this as a charge, and I have tried to carry it out as one. For two and a half years I have preached priests' days of recollection in some thirty different deaneries. By agreement with the dean, the afternoon discussion, usually a very animated one, covered such questions as: religious in the diocese, their number, the congregations to which they belonged, the religious life, the crisis in vocations, its causes and remedies. How attentive and receptive these fellow priests have been, young, not so young and old, interested in a subject which in the majority of cases an overburdened ministry had not always left them time to think about.

Have I met with at least partial success? I do not know, and it is not necessary that I should know. God requires from any of us only the effort and the good will. The results will show in good time.

But a fellow priest whom I had not met since my appointment made the following remark last autumn. It concerns the work which I have still to do, rather than that which I have done, or tried to do: 'When I heard that you were leaving your parish to do what you are doing, I said: "He is mad"; and I was not the only one to say so. But I understand now.' Many others understand, too, and more will understand, especially the young ones who are approaching the priesthood.

In the past, when the need was not felt because religious vocations were abundant and readily forthcoming, secular priests received only some very brief and sketchy information on the religious life during their time at the seminary. Could not this congress formulate the wish that the seminary course in pastoral work should include some well documented, detailed and profound instruction on this subject, where this is not already the custom? Here are the young priests who will be in charge of youth work. They are usually more in touch with young people through the various activities and movements than the older priests. It is to them especially that boys and girls will come for confession and direction. It is important for them to have some right ideas about the religious life before beginning their ministry.

Forgive me for labouring this point, but I am convinced that the instrumentality of the priest is essential and has a preponderant influence in the discovery, growth and development of religious vocations.

From my contacts with religious, I received the impression that although retreats, recollection days, conferences, undoubtedly bear fruit a friendly chat in the course of an unexpected visit, or an informal pastoral call, do so as well. It is then that the priest will find an opportunity, in the confidences given, for saying many things. Nor must we forget that the religious herself can do much to awaken and foster vocations among young people through her contact with them in her work. Her conduct, more than her words, ought to make the religious life known, esteemed and, perhaps, desired.

Some religious are occasionally lacking in tact, in discretion, in this respect, and are importunate to the point of exasperation. But are there not still more who are afraid to speak about it, who are too reserved because they are afraid of infringing the canons of personal freedom, or of seeming to apply pressure, or because they are afraid of mishandling the matter, so overwhelmed are they by the feeling that public opinion is not favourable to the religious life?

The religious, whatever her age or situation, is neither the prison gate, a weeping willow nor Cerberus; and she ought to be, or to strive to become, fraternal with her sisters, maternal with the young, frank, understanding and cheerful with everyone.

'A smiling face is an appeal in itself' because it is the outward sign of interior peace and disinterested charity.

'When you see the sister who receives you so cheerfully, it makes you want to be like her.'

To be glad to see people, to be always available, is not always easy, but it is important, and it is possible if one's whole life is founded on faith.

Fraternal charity and harmony within a community, especially if it is a small one; the joy reigning there; devotion to others—this perhaps most of all—these seem to be the essential virtues which our Lord uses to raise up vocations, because they demand tireless vigilance over self, great consideration for others, constant effort and utter renunciation. These things are a witness, the best possible witness, to the religious life and its excellence.

Most modern girls are not easy to understand; and if we are going to help them a knowledge of psychology is necessary, and above all great tact, true charity and tremendous patience. The most generous are often the most demanding, with all that unwillingness to compromise which is so characteristic of youth. They find it difficult to tolerate imperfections . . . in others.

How sad it is, and how surprising, to hear a young girl say: 'Yes, it would be right for me to become a religious, but not in that congregation'. And it is precisely that congregation which has given the girl her education, and with whose religious she has been in closest contact. Often she judges only by appearances, from the outside, superficially and without much reflection. If she knew them better, more thoroughly, she would probably think differently.

Of course, the interior life must be looked after for it is the essential thing, the thing that God loves, and on which he judges us; but outward appearances must not be neglected for it is by what our fellow-creatures see of us that they are attracted or repelled; it is by these that they judge us.

Religious who are ready to accept all the factors which can favour the Lord's call, will know that it is not only what they themselves do that counts: they must understand and value the activity of others. Are they in a state of prayer, true prayer, which the Lord hears and grants because it is after his own heart? 'Ask, and it shall be given you.'

We have followed one of the suggestions of the Pontifical Organisation for Religious Vocations. With the approval and encouragement of H.E. Cardinal Gerlier, we have just established at Lyon a chain of continuous prayer for religious vocations. It has been put to every religious community in the diocese and consists in offering, on one day each month, prayers, works and sacrifices specially for this intention. The monasteries and Mother houses within the diocese are informed of the day which has been allotted to them, the monasteries in fact duplicating for the obviously weaker congregations. Other congregations, whose Mother house is outside the diocese, but who have some religious working in it, have been asked to allow them to take part in this chain of prayer. Some have picked their own day, but the majority have just asked to be allotted one.

This scheme has served, first, as a reminder of the existence of the Pontifical Organisation for Religious Vocations. Only a few congregations are affiliated to it. But the replies we have received all say how pleased they are with the scheme, and hope that the congregations will join in this unanimous prayer.

I have a feeling that it has also broken down a certain amount of that egotistical individualism in which some congregations, more seriously affected by lack or scarcity of novices and postulants, had tended to shut themselves up.

They have become aware of participating in an activity of the Church through fraternal union in this prayer for a cause so dear to all.

I quote this at random from my correspondence:

'Thank you for this excellent scheme for intensified and collective prayer.

The Pontifical Organisation for Religious Vocations is a work in which each congregation has a particular interest from its own point of view, but we should see it above all as a work of the Church as such, which asks us to think of the needs of the entire Church.

We consider it a duty to pray for recruitment to every religious order: a duty of gratitude towards the God who consents to send us vocations; a duty of mutual help so that there may be labourers in all sectors of the Kingdom of God. Unity is strength, and through this united prayer we shall win grace to enlighten and strengthen souls, so that they may respond in great numbers to the Divine Call.'

I believe this collective, united, fraternal prayer for vocations will benefit the congregations and the activities they undertake. The latter will receive the many worthy labourers necessary for their functioning and their apostolic expansion.

And they also will benefit those who are responsible for awakening vocations, and of watching over their development, of advising and guiding them; and those families too, Christian or not so Christian, from whom God will be pleased to choose them.

At the vantage point where diocesan authority has placed him, in contact with religious, clergy and faithful laity, the Diocesan Director of Religious is at a post where he may listen and observe. His role is one of service.

On this very special point of religious vocations, which is not his whole field of work, he must respectfully inform authority of everything he observes; he must give fraternal help to his brethren the parish priests, curates, and chaplains, so that they may see clearly and act rightly; finally, he must give fatherly advice and encouragement to religious, so that by a consecrated life authentically lived, they will be worthy of those indispensable companions in that institution of the Church, the religious life.

CANON DEVAY,
Diocesan Director of Religious (Lyon)

CHAPTER XIII

THE PONTIFICAL ORGANISATION FOR RELIGIOUS VOCATIONS[1]

AN EXPLANATION OF the wording of this title may not be out of place.

The term Organisation (Opus) was chosen advisedly. It is in fact a very general term, and indicates that we are not here concerned with some association of the faithful, some pious union or confraternity. Such associations are governed by the Code of Canon Law (III P., tit. XVIII and XIX). The organisation we are to speak about does not fall into this category. This gives it the advantage, among others, of being able to admit to membership private individuals, as well as institutions of the most diverse character, families, colleges, monasteries, cities, countries and so on, and to extend to its adherents the spiritual favours which have been or will be granted to it.

This Organisation is pontifical in its very origin. It was established by the *Motu proprio* of Pius XII on 11th February, 1955. The title of *Opus primaria* and *princeps* bestowed on it by the Pontifical document is justified by the very extensive faculties granted to it for accepting aherents (can. 720–725).

It is not, however, a tribunal or official organ of the Holy See, such as the Sacred Congregation of Religious. It is an organisation attached to this Sacred Congregation, functioning under its direction and control. This is in conformity with the provisions of the Law (can. 251, par. 1).

The words religious vocations, as the text of the *Motu proprio* makes clear, must be taken in a broad sense to include all the various states of perfection recognised by the Church: *ad perfectionis christianae status vocationes*. You will be aware that there are today three canonical states or, if you prefer, three channels into which the pursuit of evangelical perfection is led:

---

[1] A booklet with this title is available from Office of P.O. of Religious Vocations, S.C. Dei Religiosi, Città del Vaticano. It contains the text in Latin and English of the *Motu Proprio*, the Statutes, Rules, Spiritual favours, etc. (Tr.)

1. The Orders and Congregations of Religion, properly so called.

2. Companies living the common life, associated with the Orders of Religion.

3. Secular Institutes.

These three canonical or juridical forms of the life of perfection have in common that they are the three official and stable ways of practising the evangelical counsels, with:

1. Statutes, solemn vows, obligatory common life in the religious state properly so called.

2. Statutes and common life in those companies without vows, which are associated with the religious congregations.

3. Statutes, but neither solemn vows nor obligatory common life, in the Secular Institutes.

The object of the Pontifical Organisation for Religious Vocations it to foster vocations to the various ways of practising the evangelical counsels which are sanctioned by the Church, i.e. vocations to the state of perfection.

No one can be in any doubt that all the redeemed are called to sanctity. 'Be you, therefore, perfect, as also your heavenly Father is perfect.' What child of God would consider himself excused from obeying this sublime injunction of the Master? This is the common vocation of the brethren of Christ, the members of his Church, for be they clergy or laity all are called to be saints.

In praeparatione animi, St Thomas goes so far as to say, men will in certain circumstances be prepared to practise the evangelical counsels. Think of the poverty which follows a reversal of fortune, the celibacy imposed by the long separation of man and wife.

It is no less true that not everyone is called to embrace one or other of the stable institutions approved by the Church in order to practise the evangelical counsels—i.e. one of the states of perfection mentioned above.

A personal call is necessary. To deny this would seem to be contrary not only to the tradition and magisterium of the Church, but also to the Gospel—the Apostolic Constitution *Sedes Sapientiae* expressly affirms it.

In the allocution on enclosure at the world Congress on the states of perfection, Pius XII on 8th December, 1950, reminded his audience that in the Latin Church priesthood *per se* did not require the practice of the evangelical counsels, apart from celibacy; and added:

'si Dei vocis invitamentum certo indicio aliquem ad evangelicae perfectionis culmen arcessit, qualibet amota hesitatione, celsi huius propositi perficiendi causa, ei proponatur libertatis libera immolatio. . . . Nemo invitus ad huiusmodi devovendi se studium propellatur, sed si id velit, nemo sit qui eum dehortetur.'

It would be difficult to find a more authoritative commentary on the challenge thrown out by Jesus to the rich young man in the Gospel.

In every age, religious vocation has been the object of the vigilant and maternal solicitude of the Church. Here again, the Enchiridion of Pontifical Documents published under the aegis of the Sacred Congregation of Religious offers an abundant collection of texts to quote. Is it not the *opus* of the Church *par excellence* to inspire, encourage, cherish and protect vocations to the religious life, by utilising to this end all the resources, means and opportunities that the providence of Christ, her Head and Spouse, puts at her disposal?

In recent times she has facilitated, with a benevolence which sometimes she has had cause to regret, the task of Christian propagandists who, assisted by all modern technical means such as radio, cinema, press, television, want to bring before the public the lesser-known aspects of the religious and even of the enclosed life.

Is it not also with a view to a more intensive cultivation, a more vigorous growth, a better yield of vocations to the organised practice of the evangelical counsels that the Church has always surrounded with jealous solicitude the birth, development and reform of religious orders, seeming to apply to herself those words of the Apostle which we read in the Common of Virgins: *Aemulor enim vos Dei aemulatione: despondi enim vos uni Viro, virginem castam exhibere Christo?* Nothing escapes her: conditions for admission; examination of candidates; their spiritual, intellectual and moral formation; the necessity for carrying out the requisite adaptations in discipline, habit, education, apostolate, conformable with the needs of souls, the requirements of the times, and with the noble desires of the young who offer themselves and aspire to evangelical perfection.

'Here are our recommendations to you yourselves', said the Pope to the Superiors General gathered together at Rome on the 15th September, 1952, 'in the present crisis in vocations: see that the customs, way of life and asceticism of your congregations do not become a barrier or a cause of frustration.'

How many new schemes and projects have been set in motion and encouraged by the Church for the benefit of vocations to the state of perfection—apostolic schools, places of instruction which are real seed beds and nurseries of religious vocations, retreat-houses where the Spiritual Exercises of St Ignatius are given, the precise purpose of which is to train souls to follow Jesus the King on the austere path of total renunciation and apostolate! The Church has never abandoned her concern for awakening, sustaining and multiplying vocations. To dissuade souls who might be called to the state of perfection from following this vocation has always been considered and denounced by her as a grave and pernicious error. We need only refer to the discourse of Pius XII cited above and the Encyclical *Sacra Virginitas*.

The Church has too much respect for Christ, her Head and Spouse, whose Spirit she possesses, too much regard for her members, knowing that every one of them is a human person called to fulfil a providential destiny *in Christo et in Ecclesia*; she is too conscious of the obligation laid on her to live in their fulness—at least in some of her members— the evangelical counsels of poverty, chastity and obedience, in prayer or the practice of apostolic charity, not to encourage and favour in every possible way those who are desirous of consecrating themselves in her, by her and for her, to these ecclesial functions as the Encyclical *Mystici Corporis* reminds us so opportunely.

The Church in fact does not merely offer to all the truth which it is her mission to teach, the grace of the sacraments entrusted to her, the priesthood of Christ and its mysterious powers which she transmits to certain of her members to perpetuate his work; she also opens schools and homes of evangelical perfection to enable those of her members called to this state to live the Christian life in its fulness (consecration and service) and in this way to grow into him who is our Head. (Eph. 4, 15).

It is this vocation, call or advancement of human beings to live the perfection of Christ himself, to integrate in their soul and in their life the two movements of the same charity which is one in its theological object: perfection and service *in Christo et in Ecclesia*, which must one day constitute the object of the Pontifical Organisation for Religious Vocations.

The diverse ways in which the practice of perfection is organised are meant to give effect to the many functions of the Church exercised by her members, among them the priesthood and other ministries of corporal or spiritual charity, in close association with the hierarchy and the whole body of Christ.

While not imposing this form of canonical life on the priesthood, the Church is not forbidden to put it before those priests who feel called to fulfil the *alter Christus* more perfectly in that way, not only in the exercise of their ministry but also in their life.

The institution of the Pontifical Organisation for Religious Vocations finds its justification, it is true, in the express will of the Holy Father, but also in the law of church life which springs from preaching of the counsels of Christ; it lays timely emphasis on the *ecclesial* character of the call to the wholeness of the Christian life: consecration and service.

It is at the very heart of the Church, within the total Christ and with consecration in view, but also mindful of a duty to be performed towards the other members of the body, that the intimate union of the religious with her Master and her Spouse, in the filial and utter detachment of love takes place. *Abneget semetispum, tollat crucem suam, et sequatur me.*

The religious institutes must never lose the sense of being an integral part of the Body of the living Church, nor yet anything evangelical they may possess.

It is for all, clergy and laity alike, to remember that the growth of a religious vocation is always for the good of the Church, and that this makes up for any apparent loss of help in a particular place, for this is apt to be judged by the lower standard of an immediate and obvious usefulness, surely less effective and far-reaching.

To ensure a supply of men for the priesthood, organisations intended to foster vocations to the priesthood have been established in numerous dioceses. In 1941 the Pontifical Organisation for Ecclesiastical Vocations was set up by *Motu Proprio* of Pius XII, and attached to the Sacred Congregation of Seminaries and Universities.

The Church, faithful Spouse of Christ and true Mother of souls, cannot forget the states of perfection instituted and organised under her care, not only as a guarantee to the faithful that the evangelical counsels will always be practised, but also to perform the numerous works indispensable to her apostolic, teaching and charitable mission. That is why, in 1916, Benedict XV extended to those activities whose object was the promotion of religious vocations the spiritual favours and indulgences granted to similar organisations in favour of vocations to the priesthood.

It only remained for this solicitude to be clothed with flesh, if one may say so, embodied in a special pontifical organisation which would be concrete evidence of the paternal and supreme care of the Vicar of Christ for souls called to the states of perfection.

The world Congress of Religious in 1950 expressed and formulated this wish. It was granted on the 11th February, 1955, when the Pontifical Organisation for Religious Vocations was born and placed under the watchful care of the Sacred Congregation for Religious.

Was there an underlying motive of centralisation and control behind it? The text of the Statutes dispels this suspicion at once. 'The Pontifical Organisation does not in any way restrict the autonomy and legitimate libery of individual societies as defined and contained in their own rules.'

One has to live and work at the very centre of the Church to see the motives which inspire and animate her in her immense task. Order, organisation, administration, law, will always remain in the eyes of the Church not ends but means, conditions more or less indispensable and necessary for a society wishing to live and progress; means ordained to a sublime end which infinitely transcends them, for it is of another order—the growth of Christ, his grace and his charity in his Mystical Body, in the members and organs which comprise it under the life-giving agency of the Holy Spirit. Order and law are and remain in the service of charity! *Finis est Caritas*.

The inauguration of the Pontifical Organisation for Religious Vocations will be for some a timely and effective reminder; for many others an encouragement, an example, a support; for all, finally, an authorised medium of information and liaison, in the service of the most noble of causes: total self-offering to Christ with a view to an official function to be performed in the Church.

There need be no fear that the two Pontifical Organisations will be opposed to each other. It is true there are two of them, but they ought not to be placed side by side or simply coupled together, as we do in the common expression: 'Vocations to the Priesthood and the Religious Life'. For they are not on the same level at all, although they are both of the Church; furthermore, they are not on two parallel planes, as has been rightly noted.

How can anyone rightly maintain, for example, that in speaking of vocations to the priesthood, only vocations to the secular or diocesan clergy are meant? None of the clergy are supposed to be unaware of the fact that priests who are members of a secular institute, such as that of the Heart of Jesus, are still really and truly secular priests and belong to the diocesan clergy. There are many French dioceses at the present time with bishops and archbishops who are members of this Institute of Perfection.

It is the purpose of the Pontifical Organisation for Ecclesiastical Vocations to promote, protect and help in every way vocations to the priestly ministry by using every opportunity to remind men of its grandeur and its necessity.

The Pontifical Organisation for Religious Vocations is concerned to encourage in every way vocations to the various forms of the evangelical life to which priests or laymen may be called (can. 107); and this, not merely with a view to fulfilling the ideal of Christian perfection, which is all for God, but at the same time to perform a work of charity, prayer or simple priestly activity within the Church.

The life of perfection organised within the Church and by the Church is offered to all, clergy and laity alike. And it would no longer be done these days to advise the layman or the priest who believed himself called to this kind of life to remain where he was, on the sole pretext that he would find the means of fulfilling his desire in his present state of life. It is for superiors and advisers to sound such souls, to examine these vocations; but no one may be inflexibly opposed to them without disobeying the Church and the solemn warning of the Pope: *Nemo invitus ad huiusmodi devovendi se studium propellatur, sed si id velit, nemo sit qui sum dehortetur* (Allocution of 8th December, 1950).

Actually, the two Pontifical Organisations are complementary. It is, in short, a question of maintaining and incessantly renewing in the Church, clergy and faithful, and, through the Church, in society, families, and in all walks of life a bright and warm atmosphere favourable not only to a normal Christian life but to the wholeness of the Christian life: perfection and service, i.e. the practice of the evangelical counsels as organised by the Church

To contribute wisely and effectively to the fostering and growth of these vocations in that immense field of the entire universe which belongs to the Father of the family, in union with all God's good workmen, is the role which has devolved on the Pontifical Organisation for Religious Vocations.

Its existence will not prevent the Sacred Congregation for Religious from exercising wisely and surely its own immediate action on the states of perfection, urging them to increase still further their power to welcome and even, if we may say so, to attract, so that true vocations to the wholeness of the Christian life may find good ground in which to grow, develop and bring forth fruit even a hundredfold, as in the parable.

As for the Pontifical Organisation for Religious Vocations, it will by its very existence be a continual reminder of the Master's invitation to a life more conformable to the Gospel, and to a more costly offering; and it will encourage by its own example the creation of similar organisations on a national, regional and diocesan level, in co-operation with the particular organisations belonging to the various institutes.

In this, as in so many other matters, collaboration and co-ordination are the order of the day. The Pontifical Organisation has the advantage of being better placed and more qualified than purely national organisations to ensure this indispensable liaison. It expects nothing more of those associations which become affiliated, particularly in the case of national organisations for religious vocations. Being an invaluable world centre of information, many matters and schemes of all kinds will thus be put within the reach and at the service of those who might wish to utilise it.

Under the terms of the *Motu Proprio* of February 1955, its principal object must be to keep in touch with national organisations for religious vocations set up or to be set up by the Councils, Conferences or Committees, of the major Superiors in different countries. Such organisations, in accordance with the wishes of the Sacred Congregation for Religious, have by now been set up almost everywhere. It is not usual for a Pontifical Organisation to interfere peremptorily in the sphere of action of the organised major Superiors, save here and there, almost reluctantly and in exceptional cases where a reminder of the necessity and advantage of the Organisation has to be given.

It is good to note that all the undertakings specified in the official document and statutes of the Pontifical Organisation are proposed to the organisations for religious vocations throughout the world, each of the organisations preserving its autonomy and liberty of action. The arranging of meetings, congresses, demonstrations, vocations days, etc., of a world-wide or international character, however, when such things are considered opportune, is the prerogative of the Pontifical Organisation, as outward manifestations of the invisible and permanent communion of souls in prayer and zeal on behalf of the states of perfection.

Even the indulgences, with which it is enriched, may be granted to present and future particular organisations of this kind because of their work, apart from their affiliation to the Pontifical Organisation, except for a few indulgences which are proper to the Pontifical Organisation, and are extended to others when they become affiliated to it.

This Pontifical Organisation is both opportune and necessary; it emphasises the traditional teaching of the Church at a time when the excellence and social utility of vocation to the states of perfection are frequently questioned. There are many misunderstandings and errors to be dispelled and the Pontifical Organisation should help bring about unity and concord in light and charity. Moreover on the practical level of recruitment conflicts of ideas, interests, influence and strategy may arise and excesses occur. A Pontifical Organisation is qualified to settle such matters with authority, so far as is possible.

It must not therefore be thought of as a sort of Office or Central Bureau for recruitment which is going to promote or publicise methods for obtaining recruits quickly and without effort.

The task assigned to it by the Pope is mainly one of instruction, of exhortation to prayer, or encouraging the faithful and the particular, by means of similar organisations in various places, those who can contribute through prayer sacrifice and action to the awakening of vocations to the states of perfection, to help in every possible way.

It will soon have its own journal or at least bulletin so that it will be able to exert, as it should, an influence which is both helpful and and worthy of its pontifical character.

The Pontifical Organisation welcomes its task, but it asks for the co-operation of all concerned, priests, religious, institutions of all kinds, to help it do a good job in the service of the Church.

GERMAIN LIÉVIN, c.ss.r.,
of the Sacred Congregation for Religious, Rome.

CHAPTER XIV

THE DOCUMENTARY CENTRE

Fr Plé found room for a paper on the Documentary Centre three years ago at the first National Conference of Priests ministering to religious, and would like this second Conference to refer to the subject again. He has, indeed, with good-will and kindness, pressed me to do this; and we are much indebted to him.

But there is no doubt that it is also his purpose to prevent the Centre from relaxing its efforts on behalf of women's vocations, especially when men's vocations tend to take up more of its working time each year. I hope that this little account of our activities since 1953 will encourage you not to lose confidence.

The report in 1953 told how we had started in 1949, following the statement from the Assembly of Cardinals and Archbishops on the *Crisis in the recruitment of women's vocations*. By 1953, in active collaboration with Fr Loret, now Secretary of the Pontifical Organisation for Religious Vocations at Rome, we had published several articles in our review, *Le Recrutement Sacerdotal*, and an entire number of this review in June 1950 was devoted to a list of the women's religious congregations in France, preceded by ten pages of practical directions for guiding vocations by Fr Loret himself.

In our annual study session for diocesan directors of organisations for vocations we had a report on women's religious vocations in 1952, and in 1953 a whole day was given to this subject.

By 1953 also we had described some schemes for edifying the faithful; parochial days of prayer for religious, watches before the Blessed Sacrament, visits to religious houses, exhibitions, days of pilgrimage with the personal testimony of religious and their relatives, retreats and vocational guidance days, tracts, papers, stories, biographies, posters, films, etc. We gave an account of the house run by the Daughters of Our Lady of Good Counsel in London[1] for girls who

[1] Vocation House, 41, Bassett Road, London, W.10.

want information about the various orders and congregations, expressed certain hopes, and prepared to published pamphlets and books.

What has happened since?

Some of these hopes, as is painfully common, have not been realised —the dream of a house in Paris like the one in London; a portrait gallery, in book form, of selected religious. When the biographer began to sketch the outlines for such portraits he found that one would require an entire volume to herself.

But the Centre has published some books, and has helped to market others. There is the brochure—16 pages well illustrated—intended particularly for young girls, with short explanations of different ways of life: marriage, a career in the social services and total self-giving and consecration to God. This has reached 250,000 copies, more than 100,000 of which have been used as a common inset for bulletins of the various diocesan organisations for vocations. It is still very much in demand.

The beautifully illustrated album in the *Fêtes et Saisons* collection entitled *Religious* has been widely circulated by the Centre in collaboration with P. Louvel.

Two editions of *Risquer sa vie pour Dieu*, a collection of twenty-odd personal testimonies concerning the origin of their vocations by young religious, published by Canon Blanadet, Superior of the Junior Seminary at Espalion (diocese of Rodez) in November 1955, have already sold out, and the book does not yet appear to have finished its career.

The Centre has also been particularly active in conducting inquiries and circulating information.

Films, too, come within its scope. To mention only those dealing with the religious vocation of women, we have in our library films made by various congregations such as *Hier, aujourd'hui, toujours*, a documentary on the Sisters of the Immaculate Conception of Castres, *Jeya, fille de Brahme*, a wonderful story about an Indian girl who had a vocation with the Sisters of St Joseph of Cluny, *Moissons tropicale*, the vocation of a young black girl to christian marriage, and yet another's vocation to the religious life with some missionary sisters, *Tokosilé la radieuse*, about a Zulu girl saved by missionary sisters, who became a Christian, then a religious.

This type of film is much appreciated in parishes and organisations.

The few copies we have are constantly travelling from one end of France to the other. The more films it possesses, the more effectively the Centre can work to bring religious vocation into greater esteem.

We are not here concerned with men's vocations, but I may say that films can do just as much for them as for the women.

In November 1955 the Centre released a film on religious vocation for children, which it had had produced through *Productions de Paris*, called *Les trois îles*. In less than a year it was shown more than a thousand times in France and abroad, either in its original version or with sub-titles. Young people under fourteen are enthusiastic about it, adults find it enlightening and instructive. The heart of religious vocation, the gift of oneself to God, the conquest of all egoism, consecration to divine charity in all its forms, contemplative, missionary, teaching, social welfare, is depicted in a most moving fashion.

It is interesting to note that, through a circular describing the scenario which was sent to almost 10,000 communities of religious women to interest them in it, to obtain their opinions and also their prayers, the Centre received effective co-operation revealed in more than 1,000 replies. Various suggestions and observations contained in these replies enabled the production committee to improve on the original draft of the scenario. Here is an instance of excellent co-operation, which is instructive and encouraging for the future.

This same film was shown in Rome in February 1956. Cardinal Feltin presided at the official première after which it was shown to the major Superiors, then to religious, then to the Regina Mundi Institute, and finally to the pupils of scholastic establishments during the week organised by Fr Loret for the Pontifical Organisation for Religious Vocations. His Eminence Cardinal Valerio Valeri, several prelates and members of the Sacred Congregation of Religious were present at one or other of these performances, and approved this work of the Centre.

But books and films are not the only means employed by the Centre to foster religious vocations. There is also a quarterly journal, *Vocations sacerdotales et religieuses*. For three years it has brought the subject of religious vocations before its readers in every number. Some of the articles that have appeared are an account of the meeting of diocesan directors, with full texts of the reports by Fr Plé and Fr Loret, Canon Arnaud and Abbé Courtois (October 1953); the report of the Conference of Priests ministering to nuns in 1953; the opening of the Higher Institute for the doctrinal instruction of religious sisters at the Catholic

Institute of Paris (January and April 1954); the text of the Encyclical *Sacra Virginitas* and of Mgr Chappoulie's pastoral Letter; the National Conference of religious sisters at Paris (July 1954); the services which enclosed nuns, teaching and nursing sisters, lay helpers, can render to the parish, by Canon Hoornaert (October 1954); the article by Dom Paul Benedict d'Asy, O.S.B. on *The Life and Future of the smaller Active Congregations* in the January, April and October numbers of 1955; news and information about the establishment of the first Carmelites at Yaoundé, the extension of the movement for fostering religious vocations in the bulletins of many dioceses, the creation of the Pontifical Organisation for Religious Vocations, the appearance of *Risquer sa vie pour Dieu*, work in connection with making the film *Les trois îles*; the constitution of the Pontifical Organisation for Religious Vocations, the National Union of the major French Superiors, details and programme of the second national Conference of priests in charge of vocations; Fr Loret's articles, *Plan de campagne en faveur des vocations féminines* and *Vocations féminine, souci d'Église*; an account of the efforts which have been made in other countries (January, April and July numbers, 1956).

By publishing these reports and articles alongside those dealing with men's vocations to the priesthood and the religious life, our concern for encouraging girls as well as boys becomes apparent—a concern which everyone, priests and laymen alike, ought to share.

This is precisely the end the Centre must strive to attain. Its business is to stir up opinion in favour of all vocations, and to offer to those who are, through their direct contact with souls in parishes, organisations, institutions, schools and movements, the immediate detectors, awakeners and guides of all those vocations, suggestions, helpful examples, methods and the possibility of instructive inquiry to assist them to perform their task well.

The Centre will do its utmost not to fall short in any way. To conclude this account, let me give you three reasons why the work of the Centre is likely to expand in the future:

(1) The fact that this project, encouraged from the start by the Archbishop of Paris and subsequently by all the bishops, and blessed by His Holiness Pius XII, although an organisation run by individuals, has been recognised by the Assembly of Cardinals and Archbishops as an organisation of the Church, and officially placed under the direction of the Episcopal Commission of the clergy, delegating its powers over

this Centre to His Excellency Mgr de Bazelaire. The constitution and work of this organisation are therefore lawfully established and are guaranteed by the hierarchy. The sole director has now had an associate appointed to assist him.

(2) What happened in 1955 at Nicolet in Canada, which we reported in the July 1956 number of *Vocations sacerdotales et religieuses* opens up a particularly interesting and fresh aspect on the constitution of a diocesan organisation for vocations, and will undoubtedly facilitate a general broadening of the common activity of those who work for vocations. Mgr Albertus Martin, Bishop of Nicolet, has set up a diocesan office under his diocesan director of vocations, comprising three sections: one for vocations to the priesthood, composed of priests nominated by himself, drawn from the seculars and the religious of his diocese and proposed by their superiors; one for brothers, composed of brothers, proposed by their superiors and appointed by himself; and one for nuns, proposed and appointed in the same way. Each section will study the problems peculiar to itself under the tutelage of the diocesan director, who, to facilitate the co-ordination of their efforts, will periodically call a joint meeting of all three sections.

On 17th June, 1956 the Bishop of Nicolet gave us permission to reprint the text of his regulations, and wrote:

'I can assure you that this work has been surprisingly fruitful: the tension which existed between the secular clergy and the religious has been speedily removed, and has been replaced by a more charitable understanding.'

(3) A simple letter written by a mother of four daughters about the attitude to women's vocations still too frequently encountered in both priests and faithful. This letter was written to Fr Bergh, who advised the writer to send it to the Centre for publication in our journal (cf pages 155–157 of the July 1956 number). It is vehement, but justifiably so; full of insight and constructive suggestions. It is worth quoting:

'During the summer holidays, I sent my girls to stay in a religious house. Until then, I had always had sufficient influence over my older girls to make them respect parochial sisters; but after the holidays I was painfully aware that their attitude had changed for the worse.

On their return, my daughters, in the middle of telling me all about the lovely walks they had had, would repeat some of the chaplain's banter about the way religious dressed, or how he would poke fun at their rule by picking on a few oddities or minor details of the religious life: I kept silent, surmising that other confidences would follow. While enthusing about a picnic which they had had in the woods with the chaplain and his mother, my eldest daughter confided that she would love to be the mother of a priest one day;

what a joy it would be, to be with her son, to help him during holidays, to watch him reach the sacred ministry and see him consecrated to the service of the altar . . . but to be a nun, or to have a daughter become one—no, never! I must have betrayed my indignation, for she went on, "Admit mother, that in the world of politics, science, the arts, sport, women play an honourable part; only the woman consecrated to God has lost the popular esteem. There are even many priests who hardly ever mention the religious life: when Jacqueline and Mlle P. entered the convent two years ago, were we even asked to pray for them?"

I was terribly hurt, and cut short my daughter's remarks. I told the Lord of my trouble: although she would be proud to be the mother of a priest one day, the gift of her whole self to God, or the gift of one of her own girls no longer meant anything to my eldest daughter.

The question of religious vocation is an extremely delicate one to broach and the world, with its comforts and gadgets to make life easy, and the lack of adaptation on the part of our religious communities are not calculated to promote the religious ideal. Many of the women's orders have preserved rules and customs dating from their foundation, often several centuries ago; but do such purely natural considerations as these justify this silence about religious vocations? Who can say what hidden, or obvious part is played by our religious communities in the life of the Church? Certainly our daughters are more precocious and very different from us, but do priests think that they are no longer capable of hearing the call of God, of giving their hearts wholly to the Lord, of turning their desires towards the Kingdom of Heaven?

Our priests, who are, alas, all too few, are haunted by the business of recruitment to the priesthood; their time is eaten into, every moment they have is taken up by one thing or another; but is there any time factor to prevent the missionary who visits the parish once a year to ask for prayers and alms for the Missions, making a charitable allusion to the effective help which our missionary sisters give in hospitals and schools? Are they so numerous that the missioner need not ask for them to be reinforced by fresh recruits? Can he not make our daughters see that pagan women and girls are also called to eternal salvation, and are waiting for them to come forward? Surely the missionary doesn't think that modern girls find travel less appealing than their grandmothers did?

Every year on the day set apart for vocations to the priesthood, the preacher, with some emotion, points out how urgently necessary it is that we should storm the throne of heaven with our prayers for vocations, and how imperative is the need for giving generously to the seminaries; but why does he not urge those of us who are mothers of families to beseech God to call our daughters to offer themselves for the sanctification of our priests and for recruitment to the ranks of the priesthood? Must St Thérèse's example remain unique, and not to be followed? And it is the man of God who, by his silence, deprives our daughters of the honour of offering themselves for such a noble cause.

The mothers of priests have often been praised, and flattered in the pulpit; many little books have been written on the priest's mother, but how many words have been addressed to the mother of a religious, who has seen her daughter cross the threshold for the last time? Are her sacrifice (infinitely more painful than that of the mother of a priest) and her generosity so insignificant that the heart of the priest has never a word of praise for her? Of course we shall be told that this is sheer pettiness and feminine jealousy, and we shall be assured that in praising the mother of a priest, the priest is associating with her the mother who gives her daughter to the Lord; but what would they think if we parents gave our offerings exclusively to women's religious communities, on the pretext that in helping the helpers of the clergy we were also supporting vocations to the priesthood?

Again, on the 21st November our priests renew their clerical promises in our parishes; but why does not the preacher who exhorts us to intensify our prayers for the clergy ask us to give a thought to religious as well, for in many communities they renew their vows on the same day?

Every year, as Christmas approaches, our priests, either in the pulpit or in newspaper articles, plead for people not to turn the anniversary of the birth of the Infant God into a purely secular festival; but what has been said or written to prevent the secularisation of our private hospitals where, because of the tragic shortage of religious, we have had to appeal to lay nurses? Who can say how many dying persons who had ceased to practise their religion have received the last sacraments, thanks to the nursing sisters?

On Mother's Day our priests have had the happy thought of celebrating a Mass for mothers, who are invited to bring their children; but why, at the end of his sermon, does not the preacher ask them to think of those who have renounced motherhood after the flesh, who have left all to devote themselves to the instruction and education of our girls, or who bring such charitable witness to our homes by nursing our sick? Is not their spiritual motherhood praiseworthy?

Could not the preacher at the May ceremonies ask the Queen of Heaven to call some of the young girls before him to take their place among the virgins who form her court?

When a girl goes to a priest to tell him that she wants to be a religious, the representative of God often comes up against the hostility of the family; but who has ever heard a sermon explaining to our parishes the importance of the religious vows? Why is this subject hardly mentioned at women's retreats? How many mothers know anything at all about the subject?

Would it not be possible to dedicate one of our Lady's feasts during the course of the liturgical year to religious? Mass would be celebrated for our religious (they are as much entitled to a Mass as we mothers of families are), and the preacher would try to explain the grandeur and beauty of religious consecration.

The writer of these rather clumsy lines realises that she is utterly unworthy of eventually being the mother of a religious. May I close with these two invocations:

Lord, give us priests, many and saintly priests, who believe in the unseen grandeur of religious vocation; priests who will make our daughters hold it in high regard and desire it for themselves.

Mary, Queen of Virgins, choose those of our daughters with ardent and generous souls, who will forget themselves and their own good, who will give themselves unreservedly to him who offered himself without measure, who will choose the good of their brethren in Christ, for his greater glory, the salvation of souls and their own sanctification.'

Mother of Four Daughters.

This letter shows that we have no right to relax our efforts on behalf of women's religious vocations, even if men's vocations do add to our responsibility!

The security which the hierarchy has given us by taking us under its wing, the example of our French Canadian brethren who have taken a broad view of the task of the diocesan organisation for religious vocations, the touching cry of this mother who does not want to see a possible religious vocation in any of her daughters stifled, makes us profoundly happy, and leads us to say:

'There is still great and fine work to be done in the Church, for the glory of God, and for an ever greater perfection of souls. Thank you, Lord, for calling us to share in it!'

CANON LIEUTIER.

CONCLUSION

CONCLUSION

I OUGHT to say at the outset that the priest appointed to give this concluding paper has unexpectedly been prevented from finishing it on his own, so these remarks are our joint effort. We shall only try to sum up some of the thoughts which have already been so well presented.

First of all, may I say what a pleasure it is to be at this Conference, after so many years devoted largely to the many problems which the religious life poses, and particularly the problem of vocation. Who in 1940 would have thought that in 1953 at St Geneviève de Versailles and in 1956 in this great hall of the Seminary d'Issy, more than two hundred priests, secular and religious, would meet to study their priestly duties with regard to the religious life of women? Who would have thought that each year thousands of religious, many of them superiors, would take part in the various conferences and days of study arranged for them, particularly in Paris?

More and more the religious sister is to be found at work in the most important fields of the Church's apostolic activity, teaching, social welfare and hospital work, parochial apostolate. You priests are continually coming into contact with her and you work in close collaboration with her. If I have not specifically mentioned the contemplative life it is only because its contact with the apostolate appears to be less direct although our duty as priests with regard to those living this life are quite as serious and perhpas find us less well prepared.

The interest shown by the Holy See and local hierarchies in many countries in the problems connected with the religious life for women is a sign that we are living in a period of great spiritual vitality, of intense missionary spirit, and that all available forces are being mobilised and co-ordinated.

We cannot help rejoice at what has been done on behalf of the religious life for women in the last decade. We have come a long way, and the future is full of hope. But you will no doubt be expecting this conclusion to remind you of the priest's duties with regard to the awakening of religious vocations in women, and to indicate some practical ways in which these duties can be fulfilled.

We must, of course, assume that the priest has grave obligations in this matter. In fact it concerns the glory of God. Those souls whom one has helped to recognise and fulfil the divine call to the life of perfect charity will glorify God by their personal sanctity; but they will also exert a powerful apostolic influence around them. Surely anyone can see that the cause of Christian perfection and of the diffusion of charity through totally consecrated souls ought to be very dear to the priest, and is rightly one of his principal concerns?

Not very long ago, in a discussion on this subject, someone asked what was the cause of all the present intense activity on behalf of the religious life. Is not the answer to be found in the fact that priests are more conscious of their really priestly tasks, and that there is a more effective co-operation with the graces of the sacrament of Order? The man of God is compelled by his very priesthood to lead those entrusted to his care to a more perfect service of God and to a whole-hearted zeal for the salvation of their brethren. Now it is in the religious life that this ideal is most perfectly realised. A real priest, athirst for the glory of God, cannot but be a convinced servant of the religious life.

What, then, are the priest's special duties with regard to religious vocation?

1. First, he must learn to understand the true nature of the states of perfection and of vocation to these states. With this in view, a systematic course in ascetics ought to be part of the syllabus in every seminary.

May I tell you a little story which illustrates what happened twenty years ago in this connection. A young priest went to see one of his friends who had become a novice. He told me: 'As soon as we spoke about spirituality the novice showed that he already knew much more about it after a year in the novitiate than I did after four years of theology!' It is highly regrettable that such a statement could be possible. But I must repeat that here also great progress has been made and things are not like this now, although we can still find examples in some dioceses.

I must stress one point—the teaching must be systematic. Otherwise it will not be really effective. Was it not with this in mind that Pius XI praised Rodriguez and his *Practice of Christian Perfection*? I do know stones were thrown at this good and holy man. One or two of his assertions are open to question, and we may well think that not all his stories to confirm doctrine have passed through the sieve of historical criticism, and many would hardly please our young people. But at least he gives a well-arranged exposition of all the principal points of a sound ascetical doctrine. And while I am speaking about systematic instruction I must point out another and still greater danger at the present day, i.e. the facility with which people fathom, or think they fathom, the various spiritualities. They all have value, when they are approved by the Church. But one must possess a general knowledge of ideas and principles to serve as the basis for a study of the various spiritualities. We meet young girls in the world who read all kinds of spiritual books containing the most diverse teaching, which many of them only really half understand, and sometimes, do not understand at all. Once, having a slight acquaintance with a certain family and knowing that one of their young daughters had entered religion a little while before, I said to the novice mistress: 'I don't expect this novice has been very easy to train.' She replied very calmly, 'Father, it didn't take long to show her how little she knew!' Evidently this novice mistress wanted to prevent a subject of quality from nourishing any illusions, without going so far as to dishearten her. So let us see that our future priests are given a systematic knowledge of the principles of Christian perfection and of the different currents of Christian spirituality.

On the nature of vocation itself we have had some wonderful new horizons opened up for us by Fr Chevignard. It takes us right into the mystery of God, who freely engraves on a creature's heart this call to belong wholly to Christ and his Church. But the question of potential vocations very quickly came up for attention. This seemed to be too ticklish a subject to be treated in passing. A short discussion proved how necessary an account of this stage was. The essential thing, i.e. that in a religious vocation God looks on a soul with a special and loving regard, has taken root so firmly that it is enough in itself to make us hold it in high esteem. Is not this total and exclusive belonging to God the highest way of fulfilling our human destiny?

Side by side with this general understanding of the nature of vocation, priests should rightly possess some knowledge, suitable to their various tasks, about the great forms of the religious life, contemplative, mixed and active. We must bear in mind, however, that it is not very easy to distinguish the two last types.

2. This obligation of learning to understand the vocation of women to the religious life will compel some priests to revise their way of thinking and speaking about it. A priest would go against the teaching of the Church if he appeared in his own teaching or direction to attribute to marriage a value equal to, or greater than, consecrated virginity. These deviations in teaching will no doubt become more and more rare in view of the Church's repeated assertions on this point, as for example in the Encyclical *Sacra Virginitas* of 25th March, 1954.

As to the manner of speaking about religious, I should like to mention a point of vocabulary. There is one expression which is frequently accompanied by an attitude, a smile if not a laugh, and that is 'the good sister'. In certain circles at any rate, these words are synonymous with a narrow-minded woman, ignorant of the things which rightly trouble the world, and whose piety is altogether too materialistic. In short, one with a narrow outlook, both naturally and supernaturally. She will be given only those jobs which do not require a very extensive knowledge. (Are there any, these days?) But one cannot expect anything of any consequence of her. It seems to me that these are certain mental associations linked with the words 'good sister'. I am told, however, that in France this expression has not always this slightly contemptuous sense. That may be so; but it might well be banished from the priest's vocabulary without loss.

The priest must in all charity learn to forgo criticism and unkind remarks about any failures to come up to the religious ideal which he may encounter. He may point out these blemishes, if it is his place to do so, to the authority which can apply the remedy; one can always inform the hierarchy if anything needs to be corrected in a particular place. But the priest must watch his words, especially with the young and with families, when speaking about what, in his own mind and with quite improper generalisation, he may sometimes call 'the narrowness of the religious life for women'. Well, it may have been narrow, and of course in some cases still is; but many nuns are now taking an increasing part, with real ability, in intellectual and social movements. You cannot speak of nuns as if they were all stupid. They are to be found at the University, and if I am not mistaken, the first woman to obtain the diploma in medicine at the University of Louvain was a nun—an example which has been widely followed, especially in missionary congregations. And what about all those who are now reading for other university degrees? At the last Congress but one of nursing sisters at Rome it was asked if, in the congregations represented there, there were any nuns who were doctors. It transpired that some of them could boast two, three, four, five, six doctors among their religious. One nun belonging to the Medical Missionary Sisters in India is a well-known surgeon.

3. After acquiring an understanding of, and personal esteem for, vocations, the priest has a duty to awaken them. How will he set about doing this?

(a) By propounding the Church's teaching on the states of perfection, in courses, sermons, retreats, whether for particular groups or otherwise. From this point of view the text of our catechisms and manuals could often be profitably expanded.

(b) By being convinced that God will bring him into conatct with souls who are called to this total fidelity. Of course, for this the priest himself must be sufficiently open to the ideas of grace to be convinced of the reality and the refinement of these divine calls.

(c) By a lively sense of the spiritual value of devotion to the Blessed Virgin and of the frequent and fervent reception of holy Communion as means of disposing souls to the total offering of themselves.

The importance of the confession and spiritual direction of children and young people will thus be clear; and also that they should belong to some organisation for spiritual training (Marian confraternities, Eucharistic Crusade) or some specialised movement of Catholic Action, etc. Religious who work with little children can often tell us some remarkable things. The ideas which these children have reflect the action of grace in innocent souls. We know well enough that moral development can be very different from purely intellectual development. Those of you who have taught in junior seminaries, for example, will be well aware that some young people, even children, have a keen sense of what is lawful and what is not, and have a real affinity with the divine. The priest who has had experience of these things will be convinced that the primary spiritual formation of a child's soul, the awakening of his desire for perfection, is a task singularly facilitated by grace. This is occasionally to be perceived very clearly. During some ceremony the collection was being taken for missions. The plate was passed to a girl of six or seven, who folded up a little piece of paper and put it on the plate instead of money. When it was opened, it read: 'I have no money at all, but I have given myself'. This should encourage us in our efforts to awaken vocations.

4. After his prayer, his teaching and pastoral work have prepared ground which is favourable to vocations, the priest must, when the decision is to be taken, watch over the choice which is going to be made. He will be sufficiently informed about possible negative pointers to be able to dissuade a young girl from a course not meant for her. He will therefore give his opinion, prudently but confidently, as to the candidate's apitude, by reference to the canonical requirements read in the light of theology.

The doctrine behind these criteria of religious vocation has been expounded. I shall only repeat one point of a directly practical nature. It may happen that in confession or in some organisation a boy or girl seems to show signs of already possessing a somewhat marked spiritual life, and we shall have to face the question: 'Might he not be called to give himself wholly to God?' Often the young person himself will raise the point: 'Father, I think I have a vocation to the religious life. What do you think?'

In such cases, a glance at the text of Canon 538, which is so sober and concise, may provide the basis for a first judgment. You know the text:

'Any Catholic, not hindered by some legitimate impediment, may be admitted to religion if his motives are right and he is capable of discharging the obligations of the religious life.'

Some prudent questions about the possibility of family difficulties, the reasons for the choice, physical and moral aptitudes, may help to make it clear that there is nothing standing in the way of a greater generosity. The confessor will encourage his penitent to foster this initial grace; and tactfully invite her to make regular use of his ministry. He will often have to help the penitent to overcome at least temporary parental opposition. Antagonism of this kind is encountered in good Christian families. It frequently springs from a false idea of vocation. I can still hear a good father of a family of ten children talking to me about one thing and another, and then, all of a sudden, the tone of his voice changed, and he said: 'Do you know what has happened to me?' I was afraid it was going to be some disaster in health or fortune. 'What's the matter?', I said. 'My eldest daughter wants to become a nun!' I looked at him, aghast. 'And you regard that as a catastrophe?' But he persisted: 'Not very long ago, I listened to a very good sermon about the duties of children to their parents!' You can see how a principle which is quite true in itself can be wrongly applied when the heart is involved. And he added: 'It would be easier for me to give my second, and she is better than the first'. This reminds me of the preacher who, in his imaginary dialogue, was trying to save Isaac. Abraham was ready to give his most precious possessions to God: 'Lord, what about giving you a hundred sheep instead of my son?' Dramatics? That may be. But it has a very deep significance for the subject we are dealing with: God is absolutely unfettered in his choice, and parents ought to think more about the signal favour of a personal call addressed to one of their children.

5. If God does him the favour of allowing him to preside in some way at the birth of a vocation authenticated by positive and negative criteria, the priest will have to continue his vigilant ministry, because this delicate flower may still be menaced a good deal before it can bear fruit. Consistent spiritual direction, training in the virtues of humility and obedience, an intense liturgical life centred on the eucharistic sacrifice—these are indispensable if the vocation is to reach maturity.

This would seem to be a convenient place to note how all these priestly duties are fulfilled to the letter by those priests who look after juniorates or similiar institutions of preparation for the religious life.

Having thus summarily reviewed the direct obligations of priests in the awakening of vocations, I must now mention a more remote, but decidely effective role: what they can do to make communities more aware of what God and the Church expect of them.

The more a community radiates charity, the more attractive it will make the religious life. This is very striking. A girl once told me that she intended to enter religion; for a long time she had felt a truly supernatural attraction for this life. But before I had time to question her she added: 'But not in *that* congregation'. 'Why not?' 'Charity does not reign in that community. I know a religious there who runs the others down.' Of course, it was not difficult to persuade her that this was only one instance. But the criticism is significant, and this girl's first reaction is self-explanatory: 'I am not going to that community because I am afraid that I should not find the authentic sign of Our Lord there'. This does indicate that, in this matter of fraternal charity, the utmost generosity is required to effect complete self-conquest.

Priests who minister to religious—and do we not all, at least occasion-ally?—must, through their teaching, administration of the sacraments, and counsel, tirelessly pursue their task of fostering the growth of charity in consecrated souls.

Charity first and foremost in a common life in which differences of character are blended into a common love of our Lord: *cor unum et anima una*. But charity also in the welcome reception of communities into the parochial and diocesan family, and the specialised movements of Catholic Action. What have we not a right to expect from these women, who are so utterly devoted both by nature and grace, when we know how, tactfully and with understanding, to integrate them into the common activity?

We can sum it all up in a few words, by adopting an idea which Fr Carpentier stresses in his recent book, *Témoins de la Cité de Dieu*: that the priesthood must take special care of this *chosen portion* of the people of God—the expression is that of both Pius XI and Pius XII—those con-secrated souls in the religious life. In doing so he ought not to be afraid that more urgent tasks will be held up. The most urgent task of all in this materialistic world in which we live is to unleash the potentialities of charity which are present in the whole Mystical Body. Where can we find elements more capable of producing a rapid and intense growth of divine charity on earth than among those souls wholly consecrated to the only Love?

Moreover, was it not written in the charter of our priesthood that priests should humbly and patiently and with supernatural devotion serve the cause of the religious life for women, on that very day when the Sovereign Priest on the Cross gave his Mother into the care of St John?

Has not our priestly life itself much to gain from this respectful contact with those who are trying to embody that spirit of humble offering shown by the Most Pure Virgin—Mother of the Divine Priest? It is so easy to be persuaded here in this Seminary of St Sulpice where we have been made so welcome these last few days. Our thoughts go back quite naturally to those conferences at the Dominican Convents at Langeac, when the Venerable Mother Agnes of Jesus launched M. Olier on his fruitful career of reforming and instructing the French clergy, and through his successors, the clergy of so many lands. We priests and religious have much to learn from each other.

Since we have established so clearly that the awakening and fostering of women's vocations is above all a work of co-operation with a prevenient grace, it is right, in concluding, that we should remind ourselves of the supreme importance of prayer in the fulfilment of this task. Furthermore, the Heart of the Sovereign Priest himself was moved by the plenteousness of the harvest and the dearth of the labourers. And we are in close union with him and with all those brave souls who await, with considerable distress, that increase for which we frequently ask in our prayer and especially at the Holy Sacrifice, more labourers for the harvest who are truly 'consecrated' to the glory of Christ and his Mother.

P. and C., S.J.